CW01123441

Traeger Grill and Smoker Cookbook: the Complete Guide. Become an Expert Pitmaster of Your Wood Pellet Grill with 365 Days of Delicious BBQ Recipes to Impress your Friends and Family

Harry Cooper

© Copyright 2020 by Harry Cooper All rights reserved.

This document is geared towards providing exact and reliable information with regards to the topic and issue covered. The publication is sold with the idea that the publisher is not required to render accounting, officially permitted, or otherwise, qualified services. If advice is necessary, legal or professional, a practiced individual in the profession should be ordered.

From a Declaration of Principles which was accepted and approved equally by a Committee of the American Bar Association and a Committee of Publishers and Associations.

In no way is it legal to reproduce, duplicate, or transmit any part of this document in either electronic means or in printed format. Recording of this publication is strictly prohibited and any storage of this document is not allowed unless with written permission from the publisher. All rights reserved.

The information provided herein is stated to be truthful and consistent, in that any liability, in terms of inattention or otherwise, by any usage or abuse of any policies, processes, or directions contained within is the solitary and utter responsibility of the recipient reader. Under no circumstances will any legal responsibility or blame be held against the publisher for any reparation, damages, or monetary loss due to the information herein, either directly or indirectly.

Respective authors own all copyrights not held by the publisher.

The information herein is offered for informational purposes solely, and is universal as so. The presentation of the information is without contract or any type of guarantee assurance.

The trademarks that are used are without any consent, and the publication of the trademark is without permission or backing by the trademark owner. All trademarks and brands within this book are for clarifying purposes only and are owned by the owners themselves, not affiliated with this document.

Table of contents

Introduction

How it works

Why pellets?

Not all pellets are the same

Pellet grill vs gas and coal barbecue

TRAEGER WOOD PELLET GRILL 101

Why choose a traeger barbecue?

How to cook at the traeger barbecue?

TIPS FOR SUCCESSFUL TRAEGER WOOD PELLET GRILLING

Choosing equipment according to your tastes

   3 different ways to grill

COMMON FAQS FOR TRAEGER WOOD PELLET GRILL

BEEF RECIPES

Beef ribs with a cabbage salad

Grilled steak salad

Entrecote in red wine marinade

Tri-tip in mosterd marinade

Floor bread filled with seasoned minced meat

Hoisin skirt steak with grilled chicory

smoked oxtail chili con carne

Seasoned roast beef on flatbread

Chili with smoked veal cheek

Caveman style veal entrecote fajitas

Grilled beef tacos with sweet potatoes

Jerky beef recipe - sweet and spicy

CHAPTER 5

PORK RECIPES

Roasted pork tenderloin

Grilled pork steaks

Grilled pork steaks 2

Grilled pork ribs

Pork with pepper, ginger and soy sauce

Pork fillet, pineapple and bell pepper shashlik

Grilled pork ribs 2

Pork tenderloin marinated with mustard honey

Grilled pork fillet with avocado salad

Pork in teriyaki sauce with vegetable salad

Mexican pork skewers

CHAPTER 6

LAMB RECIPES

Pork ribs with honey and spices

Cajun meat steak

Bbq pork ribs

Grilled lamb

Grilled leg of lamb

Lamb marinated in anchovy sauce

Grilled leg of lamb 2

Lamb chops in lemon-garlic marinade

Grilled lamb 2

Lamb cutlet burgers

Lamb with mint and bell pepper

Lamb with yoghurt sauce

Lamb cutlets with eggplant

Grilled lamb with parsley and rosemary

Lamb with lemon and oregano

Fried lamb with eggplant and red cabbage salad

Lamb and vegetable kebabs

Lamb loin in garlic-lime marinade, grilled

Barbecue chicken legs

California grilled chicken

Grilled chicken

Chicken with bbq sauce

Chicken burgers recipe

Cuban grilled chicken with salsa fresca

Asian chicken skewers

Mexican chicken skewers

Oriental chicken drumsticks

Tandoori chicken with grilled spices

CHAPTER 8

FISH AND SEAFOOD RECIPES

Small grilled red mullet with seaweed

Bbq oysters

Grilled shrimps in aromatic marinade

Grilled shrimp with mint sauce

Grilled sea bass with vegetables

Grilled lobster tails

Rib-eye smoked as a whole with smoked aubergines

Organic beef pastrami

Ikan panggang (Indonesian grilled fish)

CHAPTER 9

GAME RECIPES

Game meat racks

Venison on the salmon board - brown trout from the embers

Side to the bone with pepper and rosemary

Recipe spare ribs

Guinea fowl stuffed with vegetables

Quail on the grill marinated with vinegar and onions

Tasty bbq ribs

CHAPTER 10

VEGETABLE RECIPES

Stuffed mini peppers

Zucchini cutlets

Grilled vegetables with herbs

Grilled potatoes and tomatoes

Sweet potato salad

Grilled green peas and champignons

Grilled vegetables and mushrooms

Grilled zucchini

Grilled vegetables with butter sauce

Eggplant salad with spinach grill

Mediterranean grilled vegetables with lemon yoghurt dressing and potatoes

Grilled fruits with caramel sauce

Grilled zucchini salad

Avocado wrapped in bacon

SOME INFORMATION

THE BARBECUE

SUMMARY AND CONCLUSION

INTRODUCTION

For over the years Traeger continues to shake up the category by remaining no one in the world in pellet barbecues.

Perfected by years of research, wood-fired cooking benefits from unparalleled culinary mastery, therefore, your traeger barbecue will transform the way you cook, with stunning results every time.

Succumb to your desire for an exceptional barbecue, with the real taste of wood fire!

How it works

An auger does move the pellets from the hopper to the burn pot inside the grill. Higher is the set temperature, greater is the number of pellets distributed in the auger. Once inside the fire pot, a hot rod ignites the pellets and lights a fire. A fan then fuels the flames, creating convection heat (like an oven) to grill your food evenly. A drip tray is then placed over the firepot, preventing food from catching fire directly on the flames, while eliminating spillage to prevent flare-ups.

1. Hopper: the flavor starts here. Just add your choice of wood pellet flavor to fuel your grill.

2. Controller: turn on the grill and set the desired temperature.

3. Auger: the industry's best drivetrain delivers hardwood pellets to the firepot.

4. Fire pot: auto-ignition starts the hot rod, which ignites the pellets and creates fire.

5. Fan: at variable speed, it lights the fire by simultaneously circulating smoke and heat around your food.

Setting up your traeger grill is as easy as an oven: digital controllers ensure constant temperatures. The new pro, ironwood and timberline series all come with compatible controllers - allowing you to adjust temperatures in 5-degree increments, thus for pure precision cooking.

Why pellets?

It has never been easier to create flavorful meals because with traeger's set-it and forget-it all you have to do is load the granules into the hopper, place the food on the grill and leave the heat on. And the smoke does the heavy lifting for you.

This is because fire brings the real flavor of your food to the fore. Cooking with 100% natural hardwood makes your best recipes even more flavorful. With traeger's 6-in-1 versatility, you can grill, smoke, bake, roast, braise and grill like a real backyard chef, and their consistently reliable fire and smoke produce consistent results, every time. From low and slow, to the hot and fast, cook it all with ease.

Not all pellets are the same

The best-selling wood-burning grill demands the best pellets on the market. The real taste doesn't happen: it's made from 100% hardwood, producing the perfect smoke. At traeger, they don't just make their own pellets; they've set the 'gold standard' in pellet production. This ensures that your fuel delivers a pure hardwood taste and incredible consistency to your cooking, day in and day out.

Fruitwoods like cherry and apple impart a milder flavor and pair well with poultry, pork and baked goods. Bolder staples, such as oak, hickory, and mesquite, are tailor-made for beef, pork, and vegetables.

Pellet grill vs gas and coal barbecue

A traeger grill offers superior taste, ease of use, and repeatable results every time you fire up. Because nothing compares to the pure, leafy flavor, their state-of-the-art controllers will help you advance your cooking skills with their precise temperature control. A simple turn on allows you to grill faster, while the convection heating process eliminates the need to keep the barbecue

CHAPTER 1
TRAEGER WOOD PELLET GRILL 101

Traeger is the inventor of the pellet barbecue. Traeger has been wildly successful in the united states since 1987. It revolutionizes the way you cook by providing an incomparable taste of wood fire with ease.

The barbecues are fueled with premium hardwoods. It guarantees the typical taste of the traeger barbecue.

Unlike other food wood pellet suppliers, traeger can ensure that no hazardous products will be used in cooking your food.

Why choose a traeger barbecue?

Flavor

The 100% natural wood pellet is the typical flavor of the traeger barbecue. Those who own a traeger are unanimous on the difference in flavor provided compared to charcoal or gas: the real taste of wood fire.

Ease

The ease of use of traeger allows you to focus on what matters most: food, family and friends. The digital control panel makes cooking easier, as easy as an oven. Whether you are perfecting a recipe or watching a game, traeger has you covered!!

Performance

The control of a constant temperature that allows you to sublimate all your dishes. D2 technology allows very fast ignition and efficient smoke diffusion thanks to the powerful fan. The wifire function allows you to change the temperature of the grill and monitor cooking times from your smartphone. Cook with confidence and get results that will wow your guests!

Multifunctional

Traeger 6 in 1: you can cook at high temperature quickly or at low temperature slowly. When you turn on your traeger, you have the power to grill, smoke, roast, braise or barbecue. Whether its pizza, homemade apple pie, prime rib or grilled vegetables, you can do it all with your traeger!

How to cook at the traeger barbecue?

The power of d2

The new generation of wood-fired barbecues is here to introduce you to a whole new palette of flavors. The technology of the d2 control panel has been designed to facilitate simple and tasty cooking. Power and precision are harmoniously combined on our barbecues. Regulated ventilation and the worm screw optimize smoke production for precision cooking.

Ultra-fast ignition which promotes efficient cooking. With the precision of the temperature, cook likes a chef every time.

The direct drive fan and the endless screw powered by a variable speed brushless motor will guarantee you precision and longevity.

Wifire technology

Wifire wireless technology elevates your kitchen to other spheres. With our very intuitive grill guide, wifire technology will help you cook by downloading over 1000 recipes, guiding you step by step through the preparation, from the control panel. By adjusting and monitoring your cooking time, it will notify you when your recipe is ready to enjoy an exceptional meal. With our traeger app, you can adapt the temperatures and monitor your cooking even from a distance.

Getting the taste of a wood fire would never have been easier!

The incomparable taste

The traeger wood-fired barbecue requires the best pellets on the market. This incredible wood smoke taste is made possible by wood pellets made from 100% natural hardwood.

Fruit woods like cherry including apple provide a smoother flavor and pair perfectly with poultry, pork and pastries. Bolder woods like oak, hickory, and mesquite are made to pair with beef, pork, and vegetables.

Combine traeger spices and pellets according to your meal to best match all the flavors!

CHAPTER 2

TIPS FOR SUCCESSFUL TRAEGER WOOD PELLET GRILLING

Some tips for successful grilling

Grilling is not synonymous with very high temperatures. Whatever the material chosen, the temperature must be adapted according to the fragility of the product. If the grill and the plancha are easier to control, this is not the case with the barbecue. Be sure to prepare the embers first before considering any cooking.

Don't make the mistake of letting your products wait in the open air while waiting for the aperitif to end and you to sit down to eat. Cooking will not prevent the risk of food poisoning. Leave the products in the fridge or in a cooler and take them out as they are cooked.

Grill, plancha or barbecue must absolutely be cleaned after each use.

Some ideas to grill

- Grill

Grilled fennel bar - sole grilled in anchovy butter - sardines and mullet - côtes lamb with garlic cream - ribs - sausages - skewers of meat, poultry and vegetables.

- A la plancha

Red mullet - lamb hazelnuts - mussels - skewers of scallops and prawns - squid - lamb fillet - veal tendrons - peppers - zucchini and other vegetables - ceps - seafood - foie gras .

- Barbecued

Spare ribs - chicken crapaudine - prime rib - rack of lamb - skewers - sausages - potatoes on the grill - whole fish - eggplant caviar

The kitchen also takes its summer quarters and like every year from the first sunny days we are taken up by an instinctive desire to eat outside! Grill, plancha and barbecue are in the spotlight, but be careful to follow a few rules.

Choosing equipment according to your tastes

What first comes to the mind when we talk about grilling is often meat! A black angus entrecote à la plancha or like here a nice rib of beef make many of us salivate, however with a minimum of know-how it is possible to cook almost everything, fish, seafood, vegetables… provided you choose the appropriate material.

3 different ways to grill

- The grill

This striated cast iron plate heated by gas or electricity which accumulates heat.

Advantages: you will get a nice marking at 10:10 and the specific taste of the grill. Quick and easy to implement.

Disadvantages: no possibility of regulating the heat, therefore to be reserved for small parts for rapid cooking such as kebabs, sausages, small pieces of meat, small fish. Large pieces must absolutely be finished in the oven as for the prime rib. Significant risk of overheating and carbonization.

- The plancha

This is a smooth, non-striated stainless steel plate heated by gas or electricity.

Advantages: it allows regulating the cooking temperature (from 0 to 300 ° c) and sometimes offers two heating zones. It is therefore possible to grill and cook at the same time. It also makes it possible to recover the cooking juices thanks to a simple deglazing. It is easy to use and clean.

Disadvantages: you will have little or no specific grilled taste, but the flavor of the products is better enhanced. You will not get this famous marking at 10:10 either, but a nice reaction from Maillard.

- **The barbecue**

It is a grill placed on a bed of embers with or without a cover. Gas or electric barbecues are more like grills.

Advantages: the most basic and the most complete of outdoor cooking methods. Thanks to its cover you can grill and finish cooking a large piece of meat or poultry. You will have a characteristic smoky taste and the possibility of playing on the taste with marinades.

Disadvantages: the temperature is difficult to control. The development of the bbq requires preparation time. Cleaning is far from fun. However, you will not have these disadvantages with the kamado joe which is a special case. More than a barbecue, it is an outdoor kitchen which also acts as an oven, the temperature of which is controllable and the cleaning very simple.

CHAPTER 3

COMMON FAQS FOR TRAEGER WOOD PELLET GRILL

Pellet grill buying guide & faqs

How we chose your selection of the best wood pellet grills

Mark - the pellet grill has only been around for about 30 years and has only attracted public attention for 10 to 15 years. As such, there are actually only a relative handful of companies that produce premium pellet grills. The number of entries on this list including the number of corresponding brands is therefore limited. In fact, it's likely that whatever list of "best grills" you read will include more or less the same brands. Again, it's not because these brands are paying reviewers not to have the competition on their lists, but simply because there are only a small number of companies doing this product well, just like there are only a limited number of companies that does well in supercars or high-end watches.

Reviews - few products tends to elicit the kind of polarizing reviews from customers like pellet grills. It's hard to understand exactly why people love or hate them, but it might have something to do with the price. If you're going to drop $8 or $ 800 on an electric pellet smoker, you want and expect it to perform flawlessly. If not, you may well turn to the internet to express your rage. With that said, we certainly do take into account what people say about their pellet grills, but at the ending of the day, as always, our opinions and choices are based primarily on our own experience with these products.

Price - let's put something aside first: there is no such thing as a "cheap" wood smoker. The price of the items on this list varies between approximately € 400 and € 1,000 and more. That's why we have our eyes open for value when we can find it. In this case, the price-performance ratio is the best price-performance ratio. It offers an irresistible mix of features at a reasonable price and the quality of workmanship guarantees that it will be on your patio for many years to come, it is a value.

Features to look for in pellet grills

When it comes to the cooking mechanics of your choice, pellet grills of meat and garden-fresh produce all share more or less the same characteristics. And of course, all the grills on our list produce exceptional results with a high degree of reliability. What often separates one pellet grill from the other is all of the features. Here are features you'll want to consider when purchasing your pellet grill, along with other practical considerations to keep in mind.

Temperature control - If you are familiar with cooking, you are aware of the importance of temperature control. Of course, you can always lay a chicken right on a campfire, and in about 10 minutes, you will be able to eat something. But will it be succulent? Will it be juicy and delicious? Of course not. It will be a charred, dry, tasteless piece of meat that no one wants. The fine temperature of your pellet grill allows you to access a wide range of culinary possibilities.

Types of temperature controllers - with the above in mind, you will probably want to learn more about pellet grill temperature controllers. Here are some basics:

- Three position regulators - when you see or hear about a three-position system, it is a system that offers low, medium including high settings. While three settings are better than what you get with charcoal, the control may not be enough for the type of cooking you have in mind.
- Multi-position controllers - with a multi-position controller, you can adjust the temperature up or down at 25-degree intervals. This provides a high degree of control than the three-position controllers, and for some people who use their grill primarily for burgers and sausages, it may be sufficient.
- Pid regulators - a pid (proportional integrative derivative) regulator incorporates digital technology to maintain a more stable temperature in the grill. Rather than having a continuous cranked auger like most other pellet grills, the pid relies on an algorithm that continually monitors internal temperatures and only releases pellets when circumstances demand it.
- Pellet capacity - no one wants a pellet grill that runs out of fuel halfway through cooking. Therefore, think about the number of people who are likely to attend your parties and meetings, and make sure you buy a grill with a large enough cooking surface

and sufficient fuel capacity to keep going until the end. The fuel capacity of the above-profiled pellet grates ranges from 9 to over 20 pounds. Make sure you choose the right capacity to meet your needs.

- Heated stand - a heated stand is a great feature to have, especially when dealing with large gatherings. You want to keep in line and make sure everyone's food is good and hot. The heating floors are perfect for this. It's also a good thing to have when someone asks me, "can you keep this warm while I go for a swim in the pool?", not all wood smokers have a heated grill. So if that's a feature you're interested in, you're not just assuming that the grill you've got your eye on will have one. Make sure to check it out.
- Searing box - in a nutshell, that's what creates these iconic grilling lines on food. Food research also offers contrasts in taste and texture that make the dining experience more complete. Searing foods can also lock in flavors and juices and prevent the meat from turning to dry ash when cooked at high heat.

Additional considerations

The ease of use of the grill - Some of the best pellet grills are basically plugged in and play business. They also feature automatic temperature control as well as automatic ash cleaning and automatic grease capture and removal. Others require a little more work. If you don't mind cleaning up any drippings or ash yourself or you don't mind buying a separate thermometer to keep the temperature inside the grill and the meat, you can save a few dollars in giving you a simpler grille.

Your budget - Since, as said earlier, pellet grills don't come cheap, you'll want to make sure that the one you've got your eyes on falls within your budget. There are a few cheaper pellet grills that aren't on this list that we wouldn't buy with someone else's money. Why? Because they're so poorly built that they're likely to collapse a year later. In this case, you require going back to your bank account to purchase another. When you are considering a grill, think about the value. In this: a slightly more expensive grill that burns pellets efficiently, is well constructed and meets all of your cooking needs is a better value than an inexpensive grill that ends up on the sidewalk a year after purchase.

CHAPTER 4

BEEF RECIPES

Beef ribs with a cabbage salad

Ribs are part of every barbecue. Firm beef ribs are an original alternative, but this recipe also works well with the well-known pork ribs. Combine this with a fresh cabbage salad and let the snacking begin!

Protein: 38.0 g

Total fat: 6.0 g

Calories: 266.0

Saturated fat: 0.0 g

Preparation 30 min.

Cooking time 200 min.

Number of persons 6 pers.

Pellets 1/3 eik - 1/3 mesquite - 1/3 pecan

Ingredients

- 4 pieces of ribs
- For the marinade: get 2 tbsp maple syrup, 2 tbsp ketjap manis (oriental sauce), 1 tbsp mustard, 1 tbsp ketchup, 1 pinch of cayenne pepper, provençal herbs
- For the salad: 1/4 white cabbage, 3 carrots, 1 small red onion, 1/2 bundle parsley, 1 apple
- For the dressing: 2 tbsp mayonnaise, 1 lime, pepper & salt

Preparation

1. Mix all the ingredients for the marinade and brush the ribs generously with the marinade. Let rest for 1 hour, or better yet, do this the day before. Place the ribs on your grill and cook slowly for 2 hours or until the temperature of the thickest meat is about 70 ° c.
2. Brush the meat regularly with the marinade in between. Wrap the ribs using aluminum foil and return to the grill until the core temperature is 95 ° c. Meanwhile, mix the ingredients for the dressing. Clean the carrots wash the white cabbage and grate everything fine.
3. Finely chop the red onion, then chop the parsley. Cut the apple into small cubes. In a salad bowl mix everything with the dressing and serve with some freshly cut ribs.

Grilled steak salad

Protein: 30.0 g

Total fat: 6.0 g

Calories: 260.0

Preparation 15 min.

Cooking time 20 min.

Number of persons 4 pers.

Pellets Mesquite

Ingredients

- 1 van entrecote 750 to 1000 gr
- Traeger "beef" kruiden
- 1 bag of rucola (small bag)
- 1 bag of young, washed spinach
- Small bowl of cherry tomatoes (halved)
- 1 red onion (thinly sliced)
- 125 gr gorgonzola
- 2 tablespoons of balsamic vinegar
- Fine oil (olive oil if desired)
- Coarse salt & black freshly ground pepper as desired

Preparation

1. A preheated traeger at maximum setting.
2. Season the steak with traeger "beef" and coarse salt to taste. Allow the begging to withdraw during the warming up of your traeger.
3. When the traeger has reached its maximum heat point, the steak is placed on the "hot spot". Bake for 10 to 15 minutes on 1 side, turn and bake the other side for 10 to 15 minutes. (times varies according to thickness and weight of your steak)
4. Remove the steak from the bbq and let it rest for 10 minutes in the aluminum foil.
5. While the steak is resting, the salad is made. Take all the ingredients for the salad, mix them and work up lightly. Finish with some oil, freshly ground pepper and coarse salt.

Tasty!

Steak smoked and grilled with chimichurri sauce

The process of smoking first and then grilling gives your steak a distinct flavor. Bet you will amaze your table guests?

Protein: 38.0 g

Total fat: 6.0 g

Calories: 266.0

Saturated fat: 0.0 g

Preparation 20 min.

Cooking time 135 min.

Number of persons 4 pers.

Pellets Pecan

Ingredients

- 4 good quality peeled steaks, sliced thick
- For the marinade: 50 cl red wine, 50 cl vegetable oil or olive oil, 1 tbsp Worcestershire sauce, 1 tbsp soy sauce, 5 crushed garlic cloves, juice of 2 limes, 1 tsp black pepper, 1 tsp coarse sea salt
- For the sauce: 1 bunch of coriander washed and chopped, 6 crushed garlic cloves, 150 cl olive oil,

50 cl red wine vinegar, juice of 1 lime, 1 tbsp red onion well chopped, 1 tsp black pepper, and 1/2 tsp salt

Preparation

1. Make the marinade with all ingredients. Arrange the steaks in a dish and cover with the marinade.
2. Let it steep in the refrigerator for 8 hours. Turn the meat regularly. Let your traeger preheat on the highest setting. In the meantime, place ingredients for the sauce in a blender and mix until smooth.
3. Once your traeger is up to temperature, grill the steaks for about 3 minutes on both sides. Remove the steak from grill and cut into 1 centimeter slices against the grain of the meat. Serve with the chimichurri sauce.

Entrecote in red wine marinade

Ingredients

- 4 thin sirloin steak
- 10 bay leaves
- 3 shallots
- 1/2 tsp freshly ground black pepper
- 1 tbsp lemon juice
- 250 ml of red wine
- 100 ml of olive oil

Preparation

1. Finely chop the shallots and garlic. Mix this with the remaining of the ingredients. Add the entrecotes and let it marinate for 2 to 4 hours when cooled.
2. Prepare a barbecue for grilling.
3. Pat the entrecotes dry with a paper towel and grill them alternately to a core temperature of 55 ° c. Then take them off the grid.
4. Sprinkle the entrecotes with a little coarse salt and let them rest for 5 minutes.

Tri-tip in mosterd marinade

Ingredients

- 1 whole tri-tip
- 1/2 tbsp coarse salt
- 50 grams of mild mustard
- 2 tbsp apple cider vinegar
- 1 tbsp onion powder
- 1 tbsp garlic granulate
- 1/2 tbsp freshly ground black pepper
- 1 tsp chili flakes
- 3 tbsp olive oil

Preparation

1. Mix all ingredients for the marinade and cut the fat down to the meat.
2. Sprinkle the meat with the salt and then coat the meat with the marinade. Cover and allow it rest in the refrigerator for 4 hours to overnight.
3. Prepare a barbecue at 150 ° c with an indirect preparation. Place the tri-tip on the grid and close the lid until the meat has reached a core temperature of 52 ° c.
4. Let the meat cool for 10 minutes and cut into nice slices at right angles to the wire.

Korean short ribs

Ingredients

- 1 kilo flank style short ribs
- For the marinade and bark
- 100 ml soy sauce
- 2 tablespoons of brown sugar
- 2 tablespoons of rice vinegar or use white wine vinegar
- 2 tablespoons of sesame oil
- 4 cloves of garlic
- 1 tablespoon of grated ginger
- 1 tablespoon of tomato paste
- 2 chilies cut into pieces without the seeds.

Preparation

1. Mix everything for the marinade inside a bowl
2. Place ¾ of the marinade in a plastic bag along with the ribs and refrigerate for at least 3 hours, ideally overnight. You keep the other part for the bark.
3. Remove the ribs from the marinade and remove the excess marinade. Pat the ribs dry by using a paper towel.
4. Grill the ribs on a piping hot medium rare barbecue for about 6 minutes per side to a core temperature of 55 ° c.
5. After the last turn, spread the bark over the ribs. And turn them over one more time.
6. Let the short ribs rest for 5 minutes

Floor bread filled with seasoned minced meat

Ingredients

- 1 medium floor bread
- 300 grams of ground beef
- 2 cloves of garlic grated
- Olive oil
- 2 teaspoons spicy steak dry rub
- 5 sun-dried tomatoes
- 100 grams of old cheese
- Handful of chopped fresh parsley
- 1 egg

Preparation

1. Put a pan on fire and put some olive oil. Fry the garlic while the oil is heating up, then add the minced meat.
2. Fill the ground beef and season it with the dry rub. When the minced meat is done, the pan can be removed from the heat.
3. Cut the top cover off the bread and take out all the bread. Crumble half in a large bowl. Add the rest of the ingredients.
4. Mix everything together well and fill the bread with the mixture. Press everything down well with the back of the spoon.

5. Put the cap back on your bread and heat the bread indirectly at a temperature between 150 and 200 ° c. The filled bread is ready after about half an hour.

Hoisin skirt steak with grilled chicory

Calories: 260

fat: 8g

carbs: 37g

protein: 16g

Ingredients

- 500 grams of skirt steak
- 2 tablespoons of honey
- 1 tablespoon of rice wine vinegar
- 2 tablespoons of hoisin sauce
- 2 tablespoons sweet soy sauce
- 100 ml sesame oil
- 2 cloves of garlic
- Coarse salt to taste
- Chili flakes
- 2 x chicory
- 2 x limes

Preparation

1. Clean the skirt steak by removing fat and membranes
2. Make the marinade by mixing the honey, rice wine vinegar, hoisin sauce, soy sauce, sesame oil and garlic cloves (grated).
3. Cut the skirt steak into strips of about 6 cm and place the meat in a bowl.
4. Pour half of the marinade into the skirt steak strips and save the rest for later.
5. Leave the skirt steak in the marinade for at least 3 hours to overnight.
6. The next day, remove the skirt steak and the remaining marinade from the refrigerator.
7. Fill the cyprus grill with a full charcoal briquette starter.
8. Cut the chicory in half and thread each on the skewers. Add half a lime at the top.
9. Coat the cutting edge of the chicory with the rest of the marinade and place the skewers in the cyprus grill.
10. Thread the skirt steak alternately on the skewers and then they can also be placed over the hot coals. Discard this marinade.
11. Let them run smoothly and coat the chicory halfway with some remaining marinade again.
12. Everything is ready when the chicory is soft and the skirt steak nicely grilled.
13. Cut the skirt steak, perpendicular to the wire, into thin strips and sprinkle the meat with a little coarse salt and chili flakes.

14. Serve with the chicory and lime.

Wagyu candied peel with japanese chimichurri

Protein: 38.0 g

Total fat: 6.0 g

Calories: 266.0

Saturated fat: 0.0 g

Ingredients

- 600 grams of wagyu candied peel
- 1 tablespoon of coarse salt
- 2 teaspoons of black peppercorns
- 1 teaspoon of garlic granulate
- 2 teaspoons of dried lemon zest
- ¼ teaspoon chili flakes
- 2 white onions
- 2 courgettes
- 1 tablespoon of olive oil
- For the japanese chimichurri
- 1 clove of garlic, finely chopped
- 1 tablespoon of rice vinegar
- Handful of flat parsley, finely chopped

- 1 tablespoon of sesame oil
- A little salt to taste

Preparation

1. Prepare a barbecue with a grill plate. This can also be a good cast iron skillet.
2. Mix the ingredients for the japanese chimichurri and set it aside
3. Mix and grind the ingredients for the dry rub
4. Cut the wagyu candied peel into a square piece (s) and sprinkle the meat with a little of the dry rub. Set the meat aside for a while so that you can continue with the onion and zucchini.
5. Cut the onions into slices of about one centimeter and stick a skewer through the slice so that all rings stay together. Then cut the slices of zucchini.
6. Sprinkle the onion slices and zucchini with a thin layer of the dry rub and grill them alternately with a little olive oil on the grill plate. When the onion is soft and the zucchini grilled a little, remove them from the plate.
7. Let the grill plate heat up again for a while and then grill the wagyu sukade alternately to a core temperature of 55 ° c and then let the meat rest for 5 minutes.
8. Cut the meat into 1/2-inch slices at right angles to the wire and serve with the japanese chimichurri, onion, zucchini and white rice.

Tenderloin wrapped in bacon with balsamic raisins

Protein: 24.0 g

Total fat: 5.0 g

Calories: 256.0

Saturated fat: 0.0 g

Ingredients

- 1 kilo beef tenderloin
- 11 long slices of bacon
- For the dry rub
- 1 tablespoon of olive oil
- 1 tablespoon of brown sugar
- 2 teaspoons of cinnamon
- 1 teaspoon of oregano
- 1 teaspoon of pimenton
- 1 teaspoon of garlic granulate
- ½ teaspoon of coarse salt
- ½ teaspoons freshly ground black pepper

For the raisins

- 500 grams of raisins
- 50 ml balsamic vinegar
- 2 teaspoons tabasco chipotle

Preparation

1. Prepare a barbecue with 2 zones with a boiler temperature of about 150 ° c
2. Pat the tenderloin dry and remove the membranes if necessary
3. Cut about 10-12 pieces of salger rope with a length of about 50 cm. Place them a distance of the width of the bacon and put a piece of bacon on each piece of string.
4. Place the tenderloin on top and wrap the bacon around the meat
5. Now tie the bacon with the butcher's twine and grease everything with the olive oil
6. Mix ingredients for the dry rub, and then sprinkle it over the bacon
7. Now put the wrapped tenderloin on the barbecue. Insert the thermometer into the meat and close the lid
8. The meat can be removed from the barbecue at a core temperature of 52 ° c. Meanwhile you make the balsamic raisins.
9. Take a frying pan and throw in the raisins. Pour in the balsamic vinegar and stir well over medium heat until the balsamic vinegar has turned viscous. Then you stir in the tabasco.
10. When the tenderloin is at the right temperature, let it rest for 10 minutes.
11. Then cut the tenderloin in the middle of the butcher twine and serve with the balsamic raisins.

Beef cheek on bread with mustard barbecue sauce and tomato

Ingredients

- 1 kilo of beef cheek
- 1 tablespoon of coarse salt
- 1 tablespoon of freshly ground black pepper
- 1 tablespoon of smoked paprika
- 2 teaspoons of garlic granulate
- 2 teaspoons onion powder
- 1 teaspoon of sugar
- 33 ml sweet beer
- 33 ml chicken stock
- 1 floor loaf uncut
- 2 beef tomatoes
- Mustard barbecue sauce
- A few slices of gruyère cheese
- 2 tablespoons of olive oil

Preparation

1. Prepare a barbecue with indirect cooking at a temperature of about 120-130 ° c.
2. Cut all membranes and the outer layer of fat from the beef cheeks.
3. Mix the parts for the dry rub and sprinkle an even layer over the meat.

4. Stick a block of smoked wood between the coals and place the beef cheeks on the cooler side of the grill. Leave them for about 2 hours to a core temperature of around 60 ° c.
5. Remove the beef cheeks from the grid and place them in an aluminum container or small baking dish that they just fit into.
6. Add 1 bottle of sweet beer and the same amount of chicken stock. Close the container tightly with a piece of aluminum foil and insert a core thermometer through the foil into the meat.
7. Put the container back on the barbecue and continue cooking until a core temperature of 92 ° c or the beef cheek has become soft.
8. Remove the beef cheek from the container and let it rest for 15 minutes. Meanwhile cut the bread and tomato into thick slices. Grill the slices of bread with small olive oil on both sides until golden brown.
9. Pull the beef cheeks apart with 2 forks and cover the bread with a thick layer of mustard barbecue sauce, a generous hand of beef cheek, 3 slices of tomato and a few slices of cheese.

Smoked oxtail chili con carne

Calories: 300

fat: 11g

carbs: 20g

protein: 29g

Ingredients

- 1 kilo of oxtail
- 2 tablespoons of pimenton
- 1 tablespoon of freshly ground black pepper
- 1 tablespoon of coarse salt
- 1 teaspoon of oregano
- ½ teaspoon of dried mustard
- ½ teaspoon chili powder
- 1 tablespoon of olive oil

For the chili

- 3 tablespoons of olive oil
- 2 large sweet white onions
- 2 peppers
- 3 chili peppers
- 3 cloves of garlic grated
- 1 tablespoon of oregano
- 1 tablespoon of allspice
- 1 teaspoon of cinnamon

- 1 teaspoon of cumin
- 800 grams of diced tomatoes
- 500 ml beef stock
- 1 glass of red wine
- 2 jalapeño peppers
- 1200 grams of various types of beans
- Extra matured cheese

Preparation

1. Mix everything for the dry rub in a small bowl. Spread some olive oil over the oxtail and sprinkle the rub over it.
2. Prepare a barbecue for smoking with a boiler temperature of about 120 degrees Celsius. Place a block of smoking wood, place the oxtail on the cooler side of the grill and close the lid.
3. Let the meat smoke for 2 hours. Cut and grate everything for the chili.
4. When the meat has smoked for 2 hours, remove it from the barbecue and place in the oven.
5. Pour little tablespoons of olive oil into the pan and immediately toss in the onion, bell pepper, chilies and garlic. Let everything heat gently until the onion has turned translucent.
6. Then stir in the oregano, pimenton, cinnamon and cumin.
7. Then the tomato, beef stock and wine can be added. Let everything heat up until it starts to simmer.
8. Add the oxtail and close the lid. Let it simmer for about 4 hours. Check it from time to time whether

there is still enough moisture in the pan. If this is not the case, then pour some water in.
9. With a fork, pull all the meat off the bones and remove the bones.
10. Toss the beans together and the chopped jalapeño peppers in the pan and let it heat through.
11. Pour the chili into a bowl and grate some cheese over it.

Hot meatballs in caveman salsa

Calories: 301

fat: 5g

carbs: 23g

protein: 27g

Ingredients

For the meatballs

- 500 grams of ground beef
- 1 small red onion
- 1 clove of garlic
- 2 teaspoons cilantro
- ½ teaspoon of dried jalapeno pepper
- 2 teaspoons of cumin
- Little bit of olive oil
- Little salt

For the salsa

- 1 red pepper
- 1 lime
- 2 chili peppers
- 1 good dash of olive oil
- 250 grams of cherry tomatoes
- 2 cloves of garlic

Preparation

1. Prepare a barbecue using 2 zones and a boiler temperature of 200°
2. Place the red pepper, lime and chilies directly on the hot coals or briquettes.
3. Turn them until they are completely black all around.
4. Remove everything from the coals and put the peppers and chilies in a sealed bag for half an hour
5. Chop the onion and then mix it with the rest of the ingredients and run it through a food processor or mortar to make it smaller.
6. Mix this with the minced meat and make small balls.
7. Place the balls in a small baking dish and pour a little olive oil over it.
8. Place the oven dish with the meatballs on the barbecue and close the lid.
9. Quarter the tomatoes and chop the garlic.
10. Remove the bell pepper and chilies from the bag and rub off the black skin.
11. Cut the bell pepper and pepper in half and remove the seeds and seeds. Cut into small pieces
12. Pour some oil inside a pan and add the garlic and tomato. Stir well and add the bell pepper, lime juice and chilies.
13. Place the pan next to the meatballs on the barbecue.
14. When the meatballs have a core temperature of 70 ° c, add the heated salsa and serve with some well chopped spring onion and a few skewers.

Skirt steak with Amsterdam onion

Calories: 300

fat: 8g

carbs: 20g

protein: 27g

Ingredients

- Skirt steak ca 500 grams
- Leftover juice from Amsterdam onions. ± 200 ml.
- 1 teaspoon chili flakes
- 1 teaspoon of sugar
- 2 cloves of grated garlic
- 1 tablespoon of olive oil
- Coarse salt

With it

- Mild mustard
- Amsterdam outings

Preparation

1. Remove webbing and large pieces of fat from the skirt steak. Cut the skirt steak into manageable parts.
2. Place the juice, chili flakes, sugar and grated garlic in a zip lock bag. Add the skirt steak and let the meat marinate for at least 3 hours.
3. Prepare a barbecue for instant cooking.
4. Spread some olive oil on each sides of the skirt steak and grill alternately for a few minutes to a core temperature of 55 ° c.
5. Sprinkle some coarse salt over the meat and let it rest while you slice the baguette.
6. Cut the skirt steak into thin slices at right angles to the wire
7. Cover each piece of baguette with 2 slices of skirt steak, some Amsterdam onions and a little mustard.

Seasoned roast beef on flatbread

Calories: 200

fat: 9g

carbs: 15g

protein: 30g

Ingredients

- 500 grams of roast beef
- 4 sprigs of thyme
- 4 rosemary
- 1 garlic clove
- 1 teaspoon chili flakes
- 2 teaspoons of black pepper
- 2 teaspoons of coarse salt

For the flatbread

- 350 grams of self-rising flour
- 1 teaspoon of baking powder
- 350 grams of greek yogurt

Preparation

1. Remove the leaves out from the fresh herbs and put them in the mortar with the other marinade ingredients. Grind everything well.
2. Cover the roast beef generously with the marinade. Wrap the meat tightly and put it in the refrigerator for at least two hours (or overnight).
3. Prepare the barbecue for indirect cooking at 180 ° c boiler temperature.
4. Remove the roast beef from the refrigerator so that it can heat up during the start-up of the barbecue.
5. Place the meat on grill rack and place the core temperature probe in front of a core of 42 ° c.
6. Meanwhile, make the dough for the flatbread by mixing the self-rising flour, baking powder and greek yogurt into a good and elaborate dough.
7. Make balls from the dough and then roll each ball into an oval of about 15 by 20 centimeters. The dough can be as thin as at the bottom of a pizza.
8. At 42 ° c core, the meat may be removed and briefly in the aluminum foil. Open the barbecue's air intake a little wider and prepare it for immediate cooking.
9. Remove excess spices from the meat with kitchen paper to prevent them from burning when grilling.
10. The roast beef goes back on the cooking grate. With regular turning of the meat, we allow the core temperature to rise to 50 ° c. Then wrap the meat loosely in aluminum foil.
11. Place the flatbread on the barbecue and bake for 2-3 minutes until the bottom has a nice brown and good

grill marks. Then fold it in half with the grilled side facing each other. Then bake both sides of the resulting sandwich on both sides. 2-3 minutes on each side, but check by looking at the color and feeling the bread.

12. Cut the roast beef into nice thin slices and put them in the bun with some lettuce and chopped carrot. Time to serve!

Chili with smoked veal cheek

Ingredients

- 900 grams of veal cheeks
- 2 teaspoons of coarse salt
- 2 teaspoons freshly ground black pepper
- 1 teaspoon of paprika
- 1 teaspoon of garlic granulate

For the chili

- 2 red peppers
- 4 large carrots
- 1 whole celery
- 1 large white onion
- 4 cloves of garlic
- 2 cans of peeled tomatoes (2 x 400 grams)
- 2 tablespoons of olive oil

- 1 teaspoon of oregano
- 2 teaspoons paprika powder
- 1 teaspoon of chili pepper. More if you want it spicier.
- 2 teaspoons of cumin
- 3 cans of beans - assorted (3 x 400 grams)
- 50 grams of pouring syrup (4 large tablespoons)
- 400 ml of water
- Pepper and salt to taste

Preparation

1. Prepare a barbecue for smoking at a boiler temperature of 120 to 150 degrees Celsius.
2. Remove the fat and membranes from the veal cheeks
3. Mix the salt, black pepper, paprika and garlic powder and sprinkle the cheeks with it.
4. Place the cheeks on the grill and close the barbecue. Smoke the cheeks for 3 hours.
5. Cut the carrots, celery, onion, peppers and garlic.
6. Remove the cheeks from the barbecue and place the oven
7. Pour a little olive oil into the pan and add all the vegetables. Stir fry until the onion has turned slightly transparent.
8. Sprinkle the oregano, paprika, chili pepper and cumin powder with the vegetables and stir well.

9. Now the tomatoes, beans, syrup and water can be added and then you add the veal cheeks. Now close the lid and let everything simmer for 2 hours.
10. After 2 hours, remove the cheeks from the liquid and leave the pan open.
11. Pulse the cheeks and keep them separate. Cook the chili until the moisture has evaporated and the chili has a fine thickness. Season with some salt and pepper.
12. Serve the chili with the veal cheeks and some sour cream, grated cheese and lime wedges.

Veal sweetbreads from the barbecue

Calories: 220

fat: 09g

carbs: 10g

protein: 29g

Ingredients

- Veal sweetbreads 400 grams
- Grill barbecue
- Scale
- Pan
- Skimmer
- Cutting boards
- Briquettes or coal
- Paper towel
- Barbecue tongs
- Water
- Salt
- Vinegar
- Oil
- Pepper
- Salt

Preparation

1. Place the sweetbread in cold water for 4 hours and change the water regularly. This is to flush out any blood that may be present.
2. Fill a pan with cold water, a dash of vinegar and a pinch of salt. The vinegar ensures that the sweetbread retains its color. Place the sweetbread in the pan and put it on the fire.
3. Let the water come to a boil and then let the sweetbread simmer for another 5 minutes.
4. Remove the sweetbread from the hot water with a slotted spoon and let it cool in a bowl of cold water.
5. There is a film around the thymus that needs to be removed. Now that we have poached him first, this will take off easier.
6. There are some fat nodules on the coarse side. We can also easily remove these.
7. When the meat has been cleaned up nicely, we place it between, for example, two cutting boards with extra weight on it.
8. In this way the last moisture is pressed out and the meat becomes firmer.
9. In the meantime, we are preparing the barbecue for grilling at a temperature of about 200 ° c.
10. After at least half an hour, we cut the sweetbreads into 1.5 centimeter slices.
11. Brush the grill grate well, wipe it with kitchen paper and then with the paper with some olive oil.
12. Place the sweetbread slices directly above the coals and grill each side for about 4 minutes. This gives

the light meat a nice grill stripe. The flesh feels delicate, so grab it gently with the tongs.
13. As soon as we have reached a core temperature of 55 ° c, it can be removed and seasoned with pepper and salt. Then it is immediately ready to be served.

Caveman style veal entrecote fajitas

Ingredients

- 2 veal entrecotes of 200 grams
- Dry rub for the meat
- ½ tablespoon of pimenton
- ½ teaspoon of garlic granulate
- ½ teaspoon of onion powder
- ½ teaspoon of coarse salt
- ½ teaspoons freshly ground black pepper

For the vegetables

- 3 peppers different colors
- 1 large white onion
- 2 teaspoons of coarse salt
- 2 teaspoons of pimenton
- 2 teaspoons of brown sugar
- 1 teaspoon of freshly ground black pepper
- 1 teaspoon of onion powder
- 1 teaspoon of garlic granulate
- 1 teaspoon of dried oregano
- 1 teaspoon of cumin

- 1/2 teaspoon chili flakes
- 2 tablespoons of olive oil
- Juice of 1 lime

Serve with

- 8 small tortillas
- Little bit of lettuce
- Coriander if you like it
- Sour cream
- Hot sauce

Preparation

1. Remove the veal entrecotes from the refrigerator and let them come up to temperature
2. Slice the peppers and onion and mix the herbs and olive oil for the vegetables.
3. Put the vegetables in a ziplock bag and add the mixture and carefully knead everything together.
4. Prepare a barbecue with a completely bottom covered with glowing charcoal.
5. Place a cast iron pan on grid and pour in some olive oil.
6. Add the vegetables and stir-fry until the vegetables have a grill edge here and there and are soft. Then remove the pan from the grid.
7. Carefully blow the ashes off the embers and pat the surface of the entrecotes dry with some kitchen paper and then place them directly on the coals.

8. Leave them like this for 3 minutes and then turn them over. Let sit for another 2 minutes and then remove from heat. Wipe the leftover charcoal from the meat and let it rest.
9. Mix the dry rub for the meat and sprinkle the veal entrecotes with it. Then cut them into thin slices.
10. Grill some tortillas briefly on the grid and place them in the pan with the vegetables.
11. Serve everything with sour cream, lettuce, fresh coriander and hot sauce.

Grilled beef tacos with sweet potatoes

Preparation 30 min

baking 30 min

maceration 8 h

servings 12

Ingredients

- Beef
- 1 lb (450 g) beef flank, cut into 2 pieces
- 1 onion, quartered
- 30 ml (2 tablespoons) of vegetable oil
- 30 ml (2 tablespoons) brown sugar

- 30 ml (2 tablespoons) lime juice
- 15 ml (1 tablespoon) soy sauce
- 1 ml (1/4 teaspoon) tabasco jalapeno sauce
- 2.5 ml (1/2 teaspoon) cayenne pepper, garnish
- 2 sweet potatoes, peeled and cubed
- 30 ml (2 tablespoons) of vegetable oil
- 12 soft corn tortillas about 15 cm (6 inches) in diameter
- 1 avocado, peeled and sliced
- Sour cream, to taste
- Hot chipotle sauce, to taste
- Lime wedges, to taste

Preparation

Beef

1. In an airtight bag or in a dish, mix all ingredients. Close the bag or cover the dish. Refrigerate 8 hours or overnight. Drain the meat and onions. Discard the marinade.
2. Place a barbecue wok on the barbecue grill. Preheat the barbecue to high power. Oil the grill.

Garnish

3. Overlay two large sheets of aluminum foil. In the center, add the sweet potatoes. Oil, salt and pepper. Close the wrapper tightly.
4. Put the foil on the grill, close the lid and cook for 20 minutes, turning the foil halfway through cooking.

Remove the sweet potatoes and crush them roughly with a fork. Keep the mashed pot warm.
5. Therefore, cook the onion in the barbecue wok until it begins to brown. Grill the meat for 3-5 minutes on each side for rare cooking. Salt and pepper. Allow the meat rest on a plate for 5 minutes. Reheat the tortillas on the grill.
6. On a work surface, thinly slice the meat. Spread tortillas with sweet potato puree. Garnish with sliced beef, onions and avocado. Serve with sour cream, chipotle sauce and lime wedges, if desired.

Veal spare ribs with cola basting sauce

Calories: 300

fat: 13g

carbs: 19g

protein: 26g

Ingredients

- 2x veal spare ribs
- Peanut oil
- Smoke wood

For the dry rub

- 4 1/2 teaspoons paprika
- 4 teaspoons of pepper
- 4 teaspoons of brown sugar
- 1 1/2 teaspoons of salt
- 1 1/2 teaspoons of cayenne pepper
- 1 1/2 teaspoons garlic powder
- 1 1/2 teaspoons mustard powder
- 1 teaspoon of cumin powder
- 1 teaspoon of oregano
- 2 teaspoons of thyme
- 1 teaspoon of cilantro

For the basting sauce

- 120 ml tomato ketchup
- 120 ml of favorite bbq sauce
- 60 ml of cola
- 1 tablespoon of honey
- 1 tablespoon of brown sugar
- 2 teaspoons apple cider vinegar
- 1/2 garlic clove
- Pepper

Preparation

1. One day or morning in advance:
2. Remove the skin from the spare ribs and cut away excessively thick pieces of fat.
3. Combine all your ingredients for the rub and mix it with your fingers.
4. Provide the spare ribs with some peanut oil and immediately apply the rub on all sides.
5. Wrap the ribs in cling film and then place them in the fridge to allow the rub to absorb.
6. Day of preparation
7. Prepare the barbecue for indirect cooking (minion method) at 120 ° c.
8. Put the spare ribs out of the fridge so that they can reach room temperature.
9. If the barbecue stays at the right temperature, the ribs can be put on it. The smoking wood can now

also be almost closed between the glowing coals and the ventilation openings at the top.
10. After about two hours, the spare ribs can be wrapped in aluminum foil. A few pieces of butter are divided over the meat side.
11. To make the basting sauce, we finely chop half garlic clove and add it with the other ingredients in a pan. Bring to the boil slowly, stirring regularly.
12. After 1 1/2 hour, the ribs are ready to be unpacked. We put them on the grill grid and coat them well with the sauce. We leave them for another 15 minutes and then they are ready to be served.

Boar shoulder on the smoker

Calories: 217

Protein: 26.1 grams

Fat: 11.8 grams

Yield 6-8 servings

Ingredients

- Shoulder of boar 4 lbs (2.2 kg)
- 1/4 cup Worcestershire sauce
- 1/4 cup soy sauce
- 2 cloves garlic, chopped
- 1/2 spoon. Dry mustard
- 1/4 cup of olive oil
- 1/2 cup red wine
- Juice of 1 lime.
- Juice of 1 lemon
- 1/2 cup orange juice
- 1/4 spoon Black pepper cracked
- 1 tablespoon chopped rosemary
- 1 tablespoon chopped sage
- 1 tablespoon chopped coriander

Preparation

1. In a huge bowl, add all ingredients except wild boar.

2. Cover and let rest 1 to 2 hours to allow the flavors to get married.

3. Place boar shoulder in a large saucepan and garnish with marinade, rubbing well in the meat. You can put it inside a ziplock bag

4. Cover and refrigerate for 4 to 6 hours. Remove the meat from the marinade, while reserving the marinade.

5. Prepare a smoking pit or electric smoker at a temperature of 250 ° to 300 ° f or according to the manufacturer's instructions, using mesquite and pecan wood.

6. Boar shoulder smoke for 3 to 4 hours or until the internal temperature reaches 165 ° f, basting with the marinade every 30 minutes. If using a rack, bake at an internal temperature of 135 - 138 ° f for medium-rare or desired cooking. Slice and serve as wild boar.

Jerky beef recipe - sweet and spicy

Calories: 217

Protein: 26.1 grams

Fat: 11.8 grams

Ingredients

- 1 lb of indoor round
- Marinade
- 1 c. Red hot sauce
- 1 c. Ground ginger
- 1/3 cup of soy sauce
- 1/2 cup teriyaki sauce
- 1/2 cup of Worcestershire sauce
- 1 c. Tabasco
- 1 c. Lemon juice
- 1 c. Tablespoon garlic salt
- 1 c. Onion powder
- 1 c. Ground pepper
- 1/2 cup of brown sugar

Preparation

1. Whisk together all ingredients (except the meat) in a large glass bowl.

2. Add the beef strips (deer, moose or other) and mix to immerse completely in the marinade. Cover including marinate in refrigerator for 24 hours. Stir a few times during marinating.

3. Remove the meat from the marinade and discard the remaining marinade. Spread the meat strips on the shelves of the smoker or hang them without touching them. Take your favorite woods for smoking.

4. Put on the smoker for 6 to 8 hours at low temperature without water tray 160f - 70c. They should remain soft enough to bend without breaking. Keep in an airtight container.

CHAPTER 5

PORK RECIPES

Roasted pork tenderloin

Calories: 200

Protein: 27.1 grams

Fat: 11.8 grams

Preparation: 15 min.

Cooking time: 45 min.

Number of persons: 4 pers.

Pellets : Cherry

Ingredients

- 1 pork tenderloin (550 to 650 gr)
- Fresh sage (roughly chopped)
- Dijon mustard (+/- 3 spoons)
- Maple syrup "maple syrop" (+/- 2 spoons)
- Freshly ground black pepper including coarse sea salt
- Apple cider vinegar
- Traeger core temperature meter
- Aluminium foil

Preparation

1. A preheated traeger at maximum setting.
2. Preparation of the glaze: mix the mustard, maple syrup, salt, pepper, apple cider vinegar and a small metal saucepan (or aluminum container). Place in the traeger and let it thicken for a few minutes.
3. Take the pork tenderloin and use half of the glaze, rub the pork tenderloin with this mixture. Season with salt and pepper if necessary.
4. Place the fillet at the level of the "hotspot" of your traeger and crust on all sides.
5. Lower the temperature to +/- 165 ° c.
6. Bake to a temperature of +/- 63 ° c, remove from the traeger and let rest for about 10 minutes under aluminum foil.
7. Cut the meat into slices. Finish with the remaining icing and drizzle over the fresh sage.

Tasty!

Grilled pork steaks

Calories: 211

Protein: 27 grams

Fat: 12 grams

Ingredients

- 3 servings
- 500 grams pork
- Salt
- Black peppercorns
- Rosemary
- 1 a tomato
- 1 clove garlic large
- Vegetable oil for lubrication

Preparation

1. Cut the steaks from a piece of meat. Season them with salt, pepper and grease with vegetable oil. Preheat the grill pan. Lay out the steaks and fry each for 3 minutes on each side, changing the pattern. At the end of frying, sprinkle the steaks with rosemary, add tomato and garlic.
2. Put the pan in the oven and on the grill mode hold it there for a few minutes to completely fry the meat.

Grilled pork steaks 2

Calories: 231

Protein: 26.1 grams

Fat: 12.8 grams

Ingredients

- 10 pork steaks 2 cm thick
- Coarsely ground red chili
- Black polka dots
- 4-5 tbsp. Olive oil
- 2.5-3 tbsp. Honey
- 5 h l dijon mustard
- 4 cloves garlic
- Salt
- 1 tbsp. Lemon juice
- 2 pinches dry oregano

Preparation

1. Grind black peas in a mortar. We washed the meat, make small cuts on the sides of the meat so that it does not bend, and dipped it with a paper towel. Salt, sprinkle with chili, then ground black pepper on both sides.
2. Making the sauce. We mix honey, mustard, lemon juice. Press the garlic through a press, add to the sauce. Stir, pour in the oil. Mix again. Put the meat inside a bowl, pour over the sauce, and sprinkle with oregano. We mix. Cover with foil, leave to marinate for an hour at room temperature and stir once a hour.
3. We heat the pan. Reduce heat to medium and lay out the meat. Fry for 4-5 minutes on each side. Enjoy your meal!

Grilled pork ribs

Calories: 221

Protein: 37 grams

Fat: 12 grams

Ingredients

- Pork ribs - 2 pcs. (4 kg)
- White sugar - 1 tbsp.
- Chili powder - 1 tbsp.
- Ground cumin - 1/2 tsp.
- Salt to taste
- Ground black pepper - to taste

For glaze:

- Maple syrup - 3/4 cup
- Chili pepper (seeded and finely chopped) - 1 pc.
- Hot sauce - 3 tbsp.
- Ketchup - 2 tbsp.
- Dijon mustard - 1.5 tbsp.
- Apple cider vinegar - 1 tbsp.

Preparation

1. Grease the grill grate with vegetable oil and turn on the grill for preheating to 150-180 degrees.
2. In a small bowl, combine the sugar, chili, cumin, 4 teaspoons of salt and 1 teaspoon of black pepper. Grate ribs with this spicy mixture and set aside.

3. When the grill has warmed up enough, put the ribs on the grill with bacon, cover, and grill the pork ribs until tender, about 1.5 hours.
4. Meanwhile, prepare the icing. In a medium bowl, combine maple syrup, chili, hot sauce, ketchup, mustard and vinegar. Continuing to grill the pork ribs with the lid closed, brush them with this glaze every 2-3 minutes, until a caramel crust forms (this will take about 15 minutes). Transfer the finished ribs to a dish, grease with the remaining icing, and allow soaking and serving immediately.

Pork with pepper, ginger and soy sauce

Calories: 222

Protein: 29 grams

Fat: 12 grams

Ingredients

- Pork meat (tenderloin) - 450 g
- Chili pepper, seeded - 1 pc.
- Garlic - 3 cloves
- Fresh ginger - 1 piece (5 cm)
- Green onions - 5 pcs.
- Olive oil - 2 tbsp.
- Soy sauce - 4 tbsp.
- Rice vinegar (or other soft vinegar) - 4 tbsps.
- Honey - 1 tbsp.
- Salt
- Ground black pepper

Preparation

1. Preheat your barbecue or grill (charcoal).
2. Finely chop the chili pepper, garlic, ginger and green onion. On a piece of meat, make diagonal cuts (up to half) at a distance of 3 cm from each other. Stir all ingredients except pork. Season with salt and pepper to taste. Brush the cooked mixture over the pork so that it falls into the cuts in the meat.
3. Barbecue the meat for about 20 minutes, turning frequently (gently). Transfer to a serving dish and leave in a warm place for 10 minutes.
4. Slice the meat diagonally (opposite) into 1 cm slices. Serve with the cabbage salad. Enjoy your meal!

Pork ribs with barbecue sauce

Calories: 122

Fat: 3g

Sodium: 48mg

Carbohydrates: 0g

Fiber: 0g

Sugars: 0g

Protein: 22g

Ingredients

- Salt - 1 tbsp.
- Ground black pepper - 1 tbsp.
- Ground red pepper - 1/2 tsp.
- Pork ribs - 3 strips (about 2.5 kg)
- Lime (cut into halves) - 2 pcs.
- Barbecue sauce

Preparation

1. Remove the film from the ribs. In a small bowl, combine salt, red and black peppers.
2. Grate the pork ribs on all sides with a slice of lime. Then sprinkle with a mixture of salt and pepper on all sides. Wrap the ribs in plastic wrap, put them in a baking sheet and refrigerate for 8 hours until they are fully saturated with pepper and salt (marinated).
3. Switch on the oven with grill function to preheat to 180 degrees. Remove the ribs from the refrigerator, remove the foil and place on the wire rack. Grill the pork ribs in the oven until brown, for about 40 minutes. Then brush the ribs with barbecue sauce and bake for another 30 minutes.
4. Serve hot fried pork ribs, drizzle with remaining barbecue sauce.

Pork fillet, pineapple and bell pepper shashlik

Calories: 122

Fat: 3g

Carbohydrates: 0g

Fiber: 0g

Protein: 22g

Ingredients

- Pineapple, canned in pieces - 230 g
- Apple cider vinegar - 2 tbsp. L + 1 1/2 tsp
- Brown sugar - 2 tbsps.
- A pinch of ground black pepper
- Pork fillet (cut into 2.5 cm pieces) - 250 g
- Bulgarian red pepper (cut into cubes 1.3 cm) - 1/2 pc.
- Bulgarian green pepper (cut into cubes 1.3 cm) - 1/2 pc.
- Cooked rice for garnish (optional)

Preparation

1. Drain the pineapple, reserve the juice. Put the pineapple inside a bowl and refrigerate. In a bowl, combine pineapple juice, vinegar, brown sugar and black pepper. Pour half of marinade inside a large plastic bag with fasteners, and put the chopped pork fillet there. Fasten the bag, shake well and put in the refrigerator for 4 hours. Cover the remaining of the marinade and refrigerate.

2. Turn on the grill to preheat to medium temperature. Remove the meat from the marinade. On metal or wooden (soaked in water) skewers, string meat, pineapple and pepper in turn. Place the pork kebabs with pineapple and pepper on the grill and cook, covered, for about 10-15 minutes, brushing with the reserved marinade and turning.

3. Serve pork kebabs with pineapple and pepper with boiled rice (optional)

Grilled pork ribs 2

Calories: 102

Carbohydrates: 0g

Protein: 22g

Ingredients

- Pork ribs - 2.7 kg
- Peach nectar - 3 cups
- Unsalted tomato sauce - 420 g
- Onions (finely chopped) - 1 glass
- Brown sugar - 1/2 cup
- Salt - 1 tsp
- Mustard powder - 1 tbsp.
- A mixture of five spices - 2 tsp
- Garlic powder - 1 tsp
- Ground black pepper - 1 tsp.
- Soy sauce - 1/3 cup
- Rice vinegar - 1/4 cup
- Spicy sauce (hot) - 2-3 tsp.

Preparation

1. In a little bowl, add brown sugar, salt, mustard powder, five spice mixture, garlic powder and black pepper. Remove fat from the ribs. Grate the ribs on all sides with a spicy mixture and put them on a baking sheet, cover and refrigerate overnight.
2. Place a container under the grill to drain the juice. Put the ribs on a wire rack, meat up and fry under a closed lid for 1.5-1.75 hours.
3. Meanwhile, prepare the sauce. In a large saucepan, combine the nectar, tomato sauce, onions, soy sauce, vinegar and hot sauce. Take the sauce to boil over medium heat, reduce the heat and simmer the sauce, uncovered, for about 50 minutes, until thickened (you should make about 3 glasses of sauce). Brush the ribs with sauce every 15 minutes.
4. Serve the ribs with the remaining sauce.

Pork tenderloin marinated with mustard honey

Calories: 120

Fat: 3g

Carbohydrates: 0g

Protein: 21g

Ingredients

- Pork tenderloin - 900 g
- Honey - 2/3 cup
- Dijon mustard - 0.5 cups
- Ground chili pepper - 0.25-0.5 tsp
- Salt - 0.25 tsp

Preparation

1. Place the pieces of pork tenderloin in a tight bag (or a suitable container with a lid). Separately mix the remaining ingredients for the honey mustard marinade with the hot pepper.
2. Set aside 2/3 cup of the marinade. Pour the remaining marinade over the meat. Turn the meat over in the bag so that it is completely marinated. Put honey marinated pork in refrigerator for at least 4 hours. Turn over from time to time.

3. Drain the marinade. Cook pork in a closed grill over medium heat for 8-9 minutes on each side (for finished meat, the juice released when piercing should be transparent).
4. Heat the remaining mustard-honey marinade sauce in a gravy boat. Drizzle over the meat when serving.

Grilled pork fillet with avocado salad

Calories: 112

Fat: 4g

Carbohydrates: 0g

Protein: 24g

Ingredients

- Pork fillet (cut into slices 2 cm thick) - 2 pcs. (400 g each)
- Red onion (finely chopped) - 1/2 cup
- Lime juice - 1/2 cup
- Chili (seeded and finely chopped) - 1/4 cup
- Olive oil - 2 tbsp. Ground cumin (cumin) - 4 tsp.

For the salad:

- Medium avocado (diced) - 2 pcs.
- Cream tomatoes (diced) - 2 pcs.

- Small cucumber (peeled and diced) - 1 pc.
- Green onions (chopped) - 2 pcs.
- Fresh cilantro (chopped) - 2 tbsp.
- Liquid honey - 1 tbsp.   Salt - 1/4 tsp.
- Ground black pepper - 1/4 tsp.   Chili jelly - 3 tbsp.
- Vegetable oil for grilling grill

Preparation

1. In a small bowl, combine red onions, lime juice, chili peppers, olive oil and cumin. Pour 1/2 cup of the resulting marinade into a large plastic bag with fasteners, and put the chopped pork fillet into it. Fasten the bag and mix its contents well. Put the bag of meat inside the refrigerator for 2 hours. Take another 1/3 cup from the remaining marinade, cover and set aside. Pour the remaining marinade inside a large bowl, put the avocado, tomatoes, cucumber, green onions, cilantro, and honey, salt including black pepper in the same place, stir, and cover and refrigerate until serving.
2. In a small saucepan, combine all the reserved marinade, 1/3 cup, and the chili jelly. Bring to a boil on the medium heat and cook, stirring occasionally, for about 2 minutes.
3. Grease the grill rack with vegetable oil and turn on the grill to preheat to medium temperature. Remove the pork fillet from the bag with the marinade and put on the grill, grill the pork without covering, for

about 4-6 minutes on each side, greasing with the contents of the saucepan.
4. Serve pork fillet with avocado and tomato salad.

Pork in teriyaki sauce with vegetable salad

Calories: 110

Fat: 2g

Protein: 27g

Ingredients

- Pork - 500 g
- Carrots - 200 g (1 pc.)
- Zucchini or zucchini - 200 g (1 pc.)
- Green beans (fresh or frozen) - 150 g
- Teriyaki sauce with honey - 50 ml
- Orange juice - 30 ml
- Olive oil - 30 ml
- Sesame - 15 g

Preparation

1. Prepare all the pork ingredients in the teriyaki sauce. Wash, peel and dry the vegetables. Do the same with meat.
2. Grate zucchini or young zucchini on the same grater in a bowl with carrots.
3. Cut the beans in half. Combine vegetables and set aside.
4. Cut the pork into small cubes.
5. String the pieces of meat on wooden skewers, previously soaked in water.
6. Brush the pork with honey teriyaki sauce and place on the grill or barbecue rack.
7. Have a grill pan, you can grill or open fire. Grill the meat for about 20 minutes until tender, brushing occasionally with sauce.
8. For dressing, combine sesame seeds, orange juice and vegetable oil. Mix the vegetables in a bowl.
9. Put the salad from zucchini, carrots and beans on a plate, add the sauce to the salad and stir. Place the pork skewer on top.
10. A delicious and nutritious pork dish is ready!

Grilled pork with mango salad

Calories: 112

Fat: 4g

Carbohydrates: 0g

Protein: 24g

Ingredients

- Natural yogurt without additives - 2 tbsp.
- Honey - 2 tsp.   Garlic (chopped) - 2 cloves
- White wine vinegar - 1 tsp
- Ground cumin (cumin) - 1/2 tsp.
- Salt - 1/4 tsp.
- Ground turmeric - 1/4 tsp.
- Garlic powder - 1/8 tsp
- Ground cinnamon - 1/8 tsp.
- Ground red pepper - 1/8 tsp.
- A pinch of ground ginger.
- Whole pork cutlets - 4 pcs. (110 g each)

For the salad:

- Large mango (peeled and diced) - 1 pc.
- Red onion (finely chopped) - 3/4 cup
- Fresh tomatoes (diced) - 3/4 cup
- Fresh chili pepper (seeded and finely chopped) - 1/2 pc.
- Lime juice - 2 tsp

- Salt - 1/4 tsp.
- Vegetable oil for grilling grill

Preparation

1. In a large plastic bag, combine yogurt, honey, garlic, vinegar, cumin, salt, turmeric, garlic powder, cinnamon, red pepper and add a pinch of ground ginger. Put pork cutlets into this marinade, close the bag, shake well and put in the refrigerator for 2 hours.

2. Meanwhile, inside a bowl, combine all the ingredients for the salad, stir and leave at room temperature for 1 hour. Then cover and refrigerate.

3. Grease the grill rack with vegetable oil and turn on the grill to preheat to medium temperature. Take the bag of meat out from of the refrigerator, remove the pork cutlets from the bag and place on the grill. Grill pork with the lid closed, about 6-10 minutes on each side (the meat thermometer should show a temperature of 80 degrees).

4. Serve pork cutlets with mango salad

Grilled pork with paprika and shallot

Tender grilled pork loin with paprika, orange and herbs. A seasonal dish to enjoy with grilled vegetables or arugula.

Calories: 116

Fat: 4g

Carbohydrates: 9g

Protein: 24g

Ingredients

Number of people: 4 people

- 1 tbsp. Tablespoon paprika sweet
- 1 sliced orange and its zest
- 1 tbsp. Tablespoons of Provence herbs
- Some Himalayan salt mill towers
- A few turns of the 5 berry pepper mill
- 3 tbsp. Tablespoon olive oil
- 1 kg of sliced pork loin
- 200 g cherry tomatoes cut in the middle
- 200 g shallots, halved
- 100 g arugula leaves

Preparation

1. Combine the paprika, orange zest and Provence herbs.
2. Season with salt including pepper and add 2 tbsp. Tablespoon oil (reserving a spoon for the tomatoes and shallots).
3. Add the slices of meat and mix so that they are well coated with the marinade.
4. On a preheated barbecue, grill the pork for 8 to 10 minutes on one side, then turn and then cook it for another 8 minutes or until cooked through.
5. While cooking, grill the tomatoes and shallots on the bbq or plancha using the reserved oil.
6. To serve, garnish with arugula leaves, tomatoes, shallots and orange segments.

Mexican pork skewers

A recipe for delicious mexican pork skewers, to be served with a salad composed of chopped green salad, sliced tomatoes, cottage cheese and corn.

Calories: 112

Fat: 4g

Carbohydrates: 0g

Protein: 24g

Ingredients

- 1.5 kg pork tenderloin
- 3 tbsp. Tablespoons mexican clever mix
- 1 dash of peanut oil
- 1 box 4/4 of corn
- 2 tomatoes
- 1 green salad
- 100 g cottage cheese

Preparation

1. Cut the pork in large pieces and marinate for 2 hours in a mixture of peanut oil, salt, pepper, and the mexican malignant mix.
2. Prepare the skewers and cook them on the barbecue or in the oven for about 15 minutes, turning occasionally.

3. Serve with a salad composed of chopped green salad, sliced tomatoes, cottage cheese and corn.

CHAPTER 6

LAMB RECIPES

Pork ribs with honey and spices

Ingredients

- 12 pork chops
- 2 tbsp. Liquid honey
- 2 tbsp. Tablespoon olive oil
- 1 tbsp. Coffee curry indian tradition
- 2 pinch ground nutmeg
- 1/2 tsp. Coffee sweet paprika
- 1 tbsp. Coffee carvi

Preparation

1. Warm the honey in a saucepan.

2. Off the heat, add the oil and spices.

3. Then arrange the pork ribs in a dish. Add the marinade, cover and let stand for 2 hours.

Cajun meat steak

Calories: 250

Protein: 30 grams

Fat: 10 grams

Ingredients

- 4 nice pork chops in the back
- 4 tbsp. Soup mix cajun bbq
- 3 tbsp. Tablespoon olive oil
- 3 tbsp. Mustard
- 3 tbsp. French tarragon

Preparation

1. In a saucepan, place 4 tablespoons of water with the cajun and olive oil.
2. Boil 3 min. Then add the mustard and tarragon. You have to get a bit thick preparation.
3. Grill the chops on each side very quickly. Then brush them with the mixture.
4. Finish cooking on the grill or barbecue or in a preheated oven th. 7 (210 °) 5 min.

Bbq pork ribs

Calories: 258

Protein: 25.6 grams

Fat: 26.5 grams

Ingredients

- 125 ml of ketchup
- 85 g of brown sugar
- 65 ml orange juice
- 2 kg of pork chop
- 1 tbsp. Savory Provence soup

Preparation

1. Grill the pork ribs over medium heat with a closed lid until the meat becomes tender, turning occasionally.
2. Meanwhile, combine the ingredients in a small bowl. Brush all sides of the ribs with the sauce during the last 20 minutes of cooking, turning occasionally. At the end of your cooking, sprinkle with the savory.
3. Serve with rice or sautéed apples.

Mexican roast pork

Calories: 158

Protein: 30 grams

Fat: 13 grams

Ingredients

- 1 roast pork (1.5kg)
- 1 mexican clever mix
- 2 cloves garlic
- 1 drizzles of olive oil
- 50 g butter
- 1.5 kg of new potatoes

Preparation

1. In an ovenproof dish, place the roast pork and sprinkle it with the mexican clever mix.
2. Add the butter cut into pieces, olive oil and crushed garlic cloves. Surround the small potatoes with the skin. Add salt and pepper.
3. Bake inside a preheated oven for 20 min at 220 ° c (th 7/8) then at 150 ° c (th.5) for 1h30.

Lamb shashlik with honey sauce

Calories: 200

Protein: 12 grams

Fat: 17 grams

Ingredients

- Boneless lamb shoulder (cut into 5 cm cubes) - 400 g
- Garlic (minced) - 1 clove
- Ground cumin (cumin) - 1 tsp.
- Dried red pepper, flakes - 1/4 tsp.
- Wine red vinegar - 2 tsp
- Honey - 1 tsp.
- Pitted green olives (chopped) - 2 tbsp.
- Fresh mint (chopped leaves) - 2 tbsp.
- Extra virgin olive oil - 3 tbsp.
- Salt to taste
- Couscous for garnish (optional)

Preparation

1. In a medium bowl, mix the chopped meat with 1 tablespoon oil, 1/2 teaspoon garlic, 1/2 teaspoon cumin, 1/2 teaspoon salt, and red pepper flakes.
2. Turn on the grill to preheat to a high temperature.

3. In a small bowl, combine the vinegar, mint, honey, olives, leftover garlic, cumin and olive oil.
4. String the meat on 4 small skewers and place on the grill rack. Fry for 4-5 minutes on each side.
5. Put the kebabs on a plate (optional - with a side dish), pour over with honey sauce.

Grilled lamb

Calories: 258

Protein: 25.6 grams

Fat: 16.5 grams

Ingredients

- Lamb steak on the bone, 2.5 cm thick - 8 pcs. (120 g each)
- Ground cinnamon - 0.75 tsp
- Ground black pepper - 0.5 tsp.
- Ground allspice - 0.25 tsp
- Ground cumin (cumin) - 0.25 tsp.
- Salt - 1/8 tsp.
- Ground red pepper - 1/8 tsp.
- Vegetable oil
- Lime wedges for serving

Preparation

1. Turn on the grill to preheat to medium-high temperature. Grease the wire rack with oil.
2. In a small bowl, combine cinnamon, black pepper, allspice, cumin, salt and red pepper. Rub the lamb steaks with this mixture on all sides.
3. Place steaks on the grill rack, cook for 4-5 minutes on each side.
4. Serve the lamb steak with lime wedges. Garnish to taste.

Grilled leg of lamb

Calories: 28

Protein: 31 grams

Fat: 16.5 grams

Ingredients

- Lamb leg - 2 kg
- A mixture of 5 peppers - 2 tbsp.
- Smoked salt (coarse salt with fried crispy bacon) - 1.5 tbsp.
- Cumin - 1 tsp
- Anchovies - 20 g
- Rosemary - 8 sprigs
- Thyme - 8 branches
- Garlic - 5 cloves

Preparation

1. Let's prepare a mixture for rubbing. To do this, heat a mixture of five peppers over maximum heat in a dry frying pan until they smell.
2. Next, grind the heated mixture of peppers in a mortar with smoked salt and 1 teaspoon of cumin. Rub the leg with this mixture from all sides. Next, we make several punctures 5 cm deep.

3. We sprinkle the leg with anchovies, garlic (cutting the cloves in half, dipping them into the rubbing mixture), rosemary, thyme.
4. Rewind with a rope and bake in a charcoal grill, in an indirect way that is, placing coals around the leg. Baked for two hours at temperature of 200-220 degrees. Next, wrap the leg in foil and leave for 15 minutes. Served with grilled bell peppers and pesto. And also with mushrooms marinated in mayonnaise, soy sauce, garlic oil, coriander. Enjoy your meal!

Lamb marinated in anchovy sauce

Ingredients

- Young mutton (lamb), tenderloin - 1 pc. (650-700 g)
- Bulb onions - 1 pc.
- Salted anchovies, in oil - 1 can (150 g)
- Capers - 2 tbsps.
- Olive oil - 3 tbsp.

Preparation

1. Make cuts on the meat crosswise, about 1 cm deep. Peel off the onion and then cut into 4 pieces. Drain the anchovies and capers. Combine the onions, anchovies, capers and olive oil in a blender until a paste. Brush the cooked lamb sauce so that

the mixture goes into the cuts. Leave to marinate inside the refrigerator for 30 minutes.

2. Preheat the barbecue or grill (there should be no flame on the coals). Roast the tenderloin at low heat for 40 minutes, turning frequently. Place on a plate and leave in a warm place for 10 minutes.

3. Cut the meat into 1cm slices. Serve with unleavened bread and herbs. You can serve chickpea sauce (hummus) with fried lamb.

4. Enjoy your meal!

Grilled leg of lamb 2

Calories: 258

Protein: 25.6 grams

Fat: 16.5 grams

Ingredients

- Boneless leg of lamb (lamb meat) - 1.3 kg
- Vegetable oil (sunflower)
- Coarse salt
- Ground black pepper

Marinade:

- Olive oil (extra-virgin) - 2 cups
- Fresh herbs (oregano, thyme, savory, parsley, rosemary), coarsely chopped - 2 cups
- Garlic, coarsely chopped - 24 cloves
- Zest of 4 lemons, finely grated
- Coarse salt - 3 tsp
- Ground black pepper - 2 tsp.

Preparation

1. Cut the leg of lamb in the middle, leaving 1 inch (2.5 cm), and open like a book. Beat to a thickness of about 3 cm over the entire surface. Mix all marinade ingredients. Leave ½ cup. Place the rest of the marinade and meat in a plastic bag and close it. Stir the contents of the bag. Leave the meat to marinate inside the refrigerator for at least 8 hours (up to 1 day). Turn the bag of meat periodically.

2. Remove the lamb out from the marinade and pat dry. Leave at room temperature for 1 hour.

3. Preheat the grill to 175-190 degrees (when you can hold your hand without discomfort over the wire rack at a distance of 10 cm for 4-5 seconds). Lightly oil the wire rack. Season the meat with little salt and pepper on both sides. Fry, pressing the tongs against the wire rack for 5-6 minutes (after 3 minutes, turn the meat 90 degrees). Turn the lamb over, brush with reserve marinade. Fry the other side for 5-6 minutes, also turning the meat 90 degrees.

4. Leave the meat for 5 minutes and then chop. Serve with the remaining marinade. Enjoy your meal!

Lamb chops in lemon-garlic marinade

Calories: 258

Protein: 25.6 grams

Fat: 16.5 grams

Ingredients

- Olive oil - 1 tbsp.
- Fresh lemon juice - 2 tbsps.
- Lemon zest, grated on a fine grater - ½ tsp.
- Oregano - 2 tbsps.
- Fresh grass or 2 tsp. Dried
- Chopped garlic - 6 cloves (2 tbsp. L.)
- Salt - ½ tsp.
- Ground black pepper - ¼ tsp.
- Young lamb loin with ribs (cut off all fat from the meat) - 8 pcs. 110-120 g each

Preparation

1. Preheat broiler or grill to medium heat.

2. Prepare the marinade for the ribs. In a small bowl, add the oil, lemon juice, zest, oregano, garlic, salt and pepper.

3. Place the ribs inside a plastic bag and pour in the marinade. Close and mix the contents of the bag. Leave at room temperature for 20 minutes (up to 1 hour).

4. Remove the pieces of meat from the marinade. Roast lamb ribs on the grill or under the broiler to the desired degree of doneness (if 4-5 minutes on each side - the meat will be fried on the outside and pink on the inside). Enjoy your meal!

Grilled lamb 2

Ingredients

- Dijon mustard - 1 glass
- Soy sauce - 1/2 cup
- Olive oil - 2 tbsp.
- Fresh rosemary (chopped) - 1 tbsp.
- Ground ginger - 1 tsp
- Garlic (minced) - 1 clove
- Boneless lamb shank - 1 pc. (2-2.5 kg)

Preparation

1. In a bowl, combine the mustard, soy sauce, olive oil, rosemary, ginger and garlic. Take 2/3 cup of this mass and refrigerate.
2. Pour the remaining of the marinade into a large plastic bag with fasteners. Clean the meat from fat and films, if any. Place the lamb in the marinade bag, shake well, close the bag and refrigerate overnight.
3. Switch on the grill to preheat to medium temperature. Remove the meat from the marinade and place on the oiled grill rack. Place the lid on the grill and then cook the meat for about 50-70 minutes (the meat thermometer should show a temperature of 75 to 85 degrees). Transfer the finished meat to a cutting board, cover with foil and let rest for 10 minutes, then cut the meat into slices and serve immediately with the reserved marinade.

Lamb cutlet burgers

Calories: 158

Protein: 26 grams

Fat: 15 grams

Ingredients

- Pita thin small - 8 pcs. (30 g each)
- Minced mutton - 450 g
- Feta cheese (crumbled) - 0.25 cups
- Ground cumin - 0.25 tsp
- Ground black pepper - 0.25 tsp.
- Vegetable oil
- Red onion (rings) for serving (optional)
- Alfalfa sprouts for serving (optional), cucumber (slices) for serving (optional)

For the sauce:

- Frozen green peas (thawed) - 2 cups
- Garlic - 2 cloves
- Fresh mint, leaves - 0.5 cups
- Olive oil - 1.5 tsp.
- Water - 1 tsp, salt - 0.25 tsp

Preparation

1. Place all the ingredients for the sauce in the bowl of a kitchen processor and grind until smooth. Set the sauce aside. Turn on the grill to preheat to medium-high temperature.
2. In a large bowl, combine the minced meat, cheese, cumin and black pepper. Divide the minced meat into 4 parts, form a round cutlet from each.
3. Grease the grill rack using vegetable oil, place the cutlets on it and fry for about 6 minutes on each side. Transfer the cutlets to the plate and rest for 5 minutes.
4. Cut each cutlet in half lengthwise. And cut each pita cake in half lengthwise, but not until the end. In the middle of each pit, apply 1 tbsp. Spoonful of sauce, put on one cutlet and a choice of onions / sprouts / cucumber.
5. Serve burgers right away.

Lamb with mint and bell pepper

Calories: 258

Protein: 25.6 grams

Fat: 16.5 grams

Ingredients

- Lamb shoulder - 4 pieces (200-250 g each, 2.5 cm thick)
- Dried rosemary - 1 tbsp.
- Coarse salt
- Ground black pepper
- Fresh lemon juice - 3 tbsps.
- Olive oil - 1 tbsp.
- Dijon mustard - 2 tsp
- Red sweet pepper, finely chopped - 1/3 cup
- Fresh mint, finely chopped - ½ cup
- Green onions, chopped - 1 pc.

Preparation

1. Preheat the grill (broiler). Rub the meat (2.5 cm thick pieces) on both sides with rosemary (¾ tsp), salt (¾ tsp), pepper (¼ tsp). Cook until desired, about 4 minutes on each side (or slightly longer until the meat is medium), turning the pieces once.

2. Combine lemon juice, olive oil and mustard. Add bell peppers, mint and green onions. Serve the roast lamb warm with the prepared sauce over the meat.
3. Pour cup water into a large skillet (to cover the bottom), add ¼ tsp. Salt. Bring to a boil. Add 3 medium zucchini, cut into circles. Cook for 3-4 minutes. Discard in a colander, transfer to a bowl. Sprinkle with 2 tbsp Chopped green onions, salt, pepper and stir.

Lamb with yoghurt sauce

Calories: 128

Protein: 26 grams

Fat: 15 grams

Ingredients

- Natural fat-free yogurt - 1/2 cup
- Chopped mint - 1 tbsp.
- Lemon juice - 1 tsp
- Garlic (minced) - 1 clove
- Salt - 1/2 tsp.
- Ground black pepper - 1/2 tsp.
- Lamb (tenderloin) - 4 pieces (250 g)
- Vegetable oil for lubrication

Preparation

1. Preheat the grill.
2. Mix the first 4 ingredients. Add 1/8 tsp. Salt and 1/8 tsp. Pepper. Refrigerate.
3. Season the meat with salt and pepper. Grease a frying pan with oil, put the lamb on it, and fry for 3-4 minutes on each side. Serve with yoghurt sauce.

Lamb cutlets with eggplant

Calories: 258

Protein: 25.6 grams

Fat: 16.5 grams

Ingredients

- Lamb mince - 500 g
- Garlic (peeled and finely chopped) - 2 cloves
- Cilantro leaves (finely chopped) - 1/2 cup
- Goat cheese (shredded) - 100 g
- Salt and black pepper to taste
- Small eggplants (cut into halves) - 16 pcs.
- Olive oil
- Natural yogurt - 140 g (1/2 cup)
- Turkish bread (sliced and fried)

- Lettuce, finely chopped chili and mint leaves for serving

Preparation

1. In a large bowl add minced lamb, cilantro, half garlic, cheese, salt and black pepper to taste, mix well. Form 4 cutlets from the resulting mass and set aside.
2. Preheat the grill to the medium heat; grease the eggplants and place on the wire rack, fry for 3 minutes on each side. Transfer to a plate, set aside.
3. Sprinkle the lamb cutlets with butter and place on a wire rack, fry for about 4 minutes on each side.
4. In a small bowl, place the yoghurt and the remaining garlic and mix well.
5. Put yogurt sauce on the slices of bread, put lettuce leaves on top, and on them put lamb cutlets, fried eggplant and chili. Decorate with mint leaves.

Grilled lamb with parsley and rosemary

Calories: 238

Protein: 26 grams

Fat: 16.5 grams

Ingredients

- Young lamb meat (sirloin) - 2 kg
- Olive oil - ½ cup, garlic - 3 cloves
- Parsley - 4 tbsp
- Fresh rosemary - 3 sprigs
- Dried chili pepper (flakes) – pinch
- Salt pepper
- Parsley (for garnish), extra virgin olive oil

For the salad:

- Cream tomatoes - 4 pcs.
- Cherry tomatoes (on a branch) - 500 g
- Yellow tomatoes (desirable) - 250 g
- Fresh basil - 1 bunch, garlic - 1 clove
- Small red onion - 1 pc, olive oil of the first cold pressing - 3 tbsp.

Preparation

1. Cut off excess fat from the meat and cut the fillet in half. In a large bowl, stir together the olive oil, finely chopped garlic, chopped parsley, rosemary leaves, and chili flakes. Season with salt including black pepper to taste. Place the lamb in the cooked marinade and rub the meat well with the mixture. Leave inside the refrigerator for at least 1 hour.

2. Preheat your barbecue or charcoal grill. Roast the lamb until the desired degree of doneness is desired (8-10 minutes on each side - the meat stays pink inside). Transfer to a plate and then cover with foil and leave in a warm place for 20 minutes.

3. Cut the tomatoes lengthwise into 4 pieces (leave the cherry tomatoes intact, with stalks), crush a clove of garlic and cut the onion thinly into rings. Stir all the ingredients of the salad, season with salt and pepper and stir gently.

4. Slice the meat diagonally and place on a platter. Sprinkle with parsley leaves and drizzle with olive oil. Serve with vegetable salad.

5. Enjoy your meal!

Lamb with lemon and oregano

Calories: 268

Protein: 31 grams

Fat: 12 grams

Ingredients

- Lamb meat (portions of 150 g each) - 4 pcs.
- Lemon juice - 1 tbsp.
- Oregano leaves - 2 tbsps.
- Garlic - 1 clove
- Olive oil - 0.25 cups
- Sea salt, ground black pepper
- Greek salad

Preparation

1. In a non-metallic bowl, stir the lamb chunks with olive oil, lemon juice, oregano, minced garlic, salt and black pepper. Leave to marinate for 30 minutes. Preheat your grill or barbecue to high heat. (how different? The grill is a round grill with a grate and lid, and the barbecue is rectangular and without a lid.)
2. Grill the meat to a desired degree of doneness (for example, 3-4 minutes on each side is enough for

meat "with blood") ... Serve the meat with greek salad (tomatoes, cucumbers, olives, red onions, and feta). Enjoy your meal!

Fried lamb with eggplant and red cabbage salad

Calories: 258

Protein: 25.6 grams

Fat: 16.5 grams

Ingredients

- Eggplant (cut into thin slices) - 1 pc. (about 300 g)
- Salt
- Young lamb (lamb) on bones (completely clean the ribs with meat from fat) - 12 pcs.
- Olive oil - 2 tbsp.
- Salt, ground black pepper

For the salad:

- Red cabbage - ½ a small head of cabbage
- Green beans (blanch and cut diagonally) - 100 g
- Small cucumber (cut thinly longitudinally) - 1 pc.
- Green onion (cut diagonally) - 1 pc.

- Small red onion (cut into thin rings) - 1 pc.
- Celery stalks (peel and cut into thin diagonals) - 2 pcs.
- Hazelnuts (or pine nuts) - 60 g
- Olive oil (first cold pressed) - 2 tbsp.
- Balsamic vinegar - 1 tsp

Preparation

1. Put the chopped eggplant in a colander, sprinkle with salt and let sit for 20 minutes. Rinse it and pat dry it with a paper towel.

2. Preheat your barbecue or grill. Brush the lamb using olive oil and then sprinkle with salt and pepper. Grill the pitted meat on a wire rack over medium heat until cooked to the desired degree (e.g. 3-5 minutes on each side). Place on a plate, cover with foil and leave in a warm place for 10 minutes. Fry the eggplant slices over high heat until golden brown (3 minutes on each side). Place on a plate and keep warm

3. Make a red cabbage salad. Chop the cabbage finely and then combine with the rest of the salad ingredients. Season with salt and pepper to taste and stir gently. Serve grilled meats with eggplant and cooked salad.

Lamb and vegetable kebabs

Calories: 238

Protein: 25.6 grams

Fat: 16.5 grams

Ingredients

- Fresh lemon juice - 1/2 cup
- Olive oil - 4 tsp
- Dried oregano - 2 tbsp.
- Garlic (chopped) - 6 cloves
- Lamb (cut into 2.5 cm pieces) - 450 g
- Cherry tomatoes - 16 pieces
- Bulgarian green pepper (seeded and cut into 2.5 cm cubes) - 1 pc.
- Salad onion (cut into slices 2.5 cm) - 1 pc.
- Vegetable oil for grilling grill

Preparation

1. In a bowl, combine lemon juice, oil, oregano and garlic, mix well. Take 1/4 cup of the marinade from the total mass for lubrication, cover and refrigerate. Pour the remaining marinade into a big plastic bag with fasteners, put the meat in the same place, close the bag and put in the refrigerator for at least 8

hours, or better for 10, periodically stirring the meat with the marinade.

2. Grease the grill grate with vegetable oil and turn on the grill to preheat to medium temperature. Remove the meat from the marinade. On metal skewers, string meat, tomatoes, onions and peppers in turn. Place kebabs on the grill and cook, uncovered, for about 3 minutes on each side. Then grease the kebabs on all sides with the reserved marinade and fry for another 8-10 minutes. Grease the finished kebabs with the remaining marinade and serve immediately.

Lamb shashlik with aromatic herbs

Calories: 260

fat: 8g

carbs: 37g

protein: 16g

Ingredients

- Lamb shank, boneless pulp (cut into 2.5 cm pieces) - 1300 g
- Fresh oregano, leaves - 0.25 cups
- Fresh rosemary (chopped) - 2 tbsp.
- Olive oil - 3 tbsp.
- Lemon juice - 1 tbsp.
- Salt - 2 tsp
- Lemon zest - 2 tsp
- Garlic (chopped) - 4 cloves
- Red onion (cut into 2.5 cm cubes) - 2 pcs.
- Vegetable oil

Preparation

1. Switch on the grill to preheat.
2. Place oregano, rosemary, olive oil, lemon juice, salt, zest and garlic in a bowl of a kitchen processor, chop.
3. String meat and onions on wooden skewers, brush with herbal mixture.
4. Grease the grill grate with oil, put the kebabs. Fry the lamb skewers for about 9 minutes, turning occasionally.

Lamb kebabs with green salad and cheese

Ingredients

- Lamb, boneless shoulder blade (cut into 2.5 cm cubes) - 400 g
- Arugula, young leaves - 110 g
- Red onion (cut into thin rings) - 0.25 cups (about 0.5 onions)
- Feta or blue cheese (crumbled) - 0.25 cups
- Lemon juice - 2 tbsp
- Sour cream - 2 tsp.
- Garlic (minced) - 1 clove
- Salt to taste
- Ground black pepper - to taste
- Extra virgin olive oil - 0.25 cups

Preparation

1. Place the rack in the oven at a distance of 10 cm from the upper heater, and turn on the oven itself with the "grill" function to preheat to a high temperature.

2. In a small bowl, add lemon juice, sour cream, garlic and a pinch of salt, gradually add 1/4 cup of oil.

3. In another bowl, mix the meat with 1 tablespoon of oil, 1/2 teaspoon of salt and 1/4 teaspoon of pepper. String the meat on skewers. Place the skewers on a grill tray, place under the grill, and fry the lamb skewers, turning, about 4 minutes on each side. Transfer the fried kebabs to a long serving plate, drizzle with 3 tablespoons of the dressing.

4. Using a separate bowl, mix the arugula with onions and dressing to taste, season with salt and pepper, mix well.

5. Place the salad on serving bowls and top with the meat skewers. Sprinkle with cheese and serve the lamb skewers immediately.

Lamb loin in garlic-lime marinade, grilled

Calories: 260

fat: 8g

carbs: 37g

protein: 16g

Ingredients

- Lamb loin - 1.5 kg
- Lime - 1 pc.
- Garlic - 2 cloves
- Olive oil - 4 tbsp. Spoons
- Coriander (seeds) - 1 tsp
- Zira (seeds) - 1 tsp
- Ground ginger - 0.5 tsp
- Freshly ground pepper - to taste
- Salt to taste

Preparation

1. Cut the lamb loin into portions (one rib at a time). We start cooking with the marinade. To do this, put coriander, cumin, ground ginger, salt and freshly ground pepper in a mortar. Grind the spices until smooth. Pass the garlic into the mortar through a press.
2. Cut the lime into 4 pieces. Squeeze juice of one quarter of the lime into the mortar. We leave the rest of the lime to serve the finished dish. Add olive oil.
3. Mix the contents of the mortar. Now we marinate the lamb. For the convenience of marinating, transfer the meat to a deep bowl. Pour the marinade over the meat. Using our hands we distribute the marinade over each piece of meat. Try to get the marinade evenly over the entire surface of the meat.
4. Leave the meat to marinate for 2 hours. If you marinate meat in the refrigerator, remove it half an hour before cooking.
5. An hour and a half after the start of marinating, prepare the grill for use. We light up coal. I do it as conveniently as possible - in a special starter. Pour hot charcoal into the grill. Install the upper grill, heat it and clean it with a metal brush.
6. Fry the lamb loin over medium heat for 2.5-3 minutes on each side.
7. Serve the grilled lamb loin on the table. Before eating, i recommend pouring some lime juice over the lamb.

Grilled lamb with spicy sauce

Calories: 220

fat: 8g

carbs: 33g

protein: 22g

Ingredients

- Brown sugar - 1 tbsp
- Salt - 1 tsp
- Onion powder - 1 tsp
- Chili powder - 1 tsp
- Paprika - 1 tsp
- Dried oregano - 1/2 tsp
- Ginger powder - 1/4 tsp
- Ground allspice - 1/4 tsp.
- Ground black pepper - 1/4 tsp.
- Lamb on the bone - 8 pieces (120 g each)
- Odorless vegetable oil
- Peach jam

Preparation

1. Inside a small bowl, combine sugar, salt, onion powder, chili, paprika, oregano, ginger powder, allspice and black pepper. With this mixture, grate the lamb on the bone well.

2. Turn on the grill to preheat to medium-high heat. Grease a baking sheet with vegetable oil. Place the meat on baking sheet and grill the lamb for about 3-4 minutes on each side, then brush each piece of roast lamb with 1 teaspoon of jam, turn over to the other side, cook for 2 minute, then brush the roast lamb again with the same amount of jam and remove from fire.

Barbecue chicken legs

Classic bbq chicken legs are juicy and tender, infused with wood-fired aromas. Serve in your backyard with baked beans and a cool beer.

Calories: 260

fat: 8g

carbs: 37g

protein: 16g

Ingredients

- 6 chicken legs with skin
- 1 jar of spice mix for roasting, grilling and barbecuing based on sweet bell pepper salt and ground black pepper

Preparation

When you are ready to cook, start the traeger grill on smoke, with the lid open, until there is a good fire (4 to 5 minutes). Set the temperature to 130 ° c and heat with the lid closed for 10 to 15 minutes. Remove excess skin including fat from the chicken legs while the grill heats up. Season with a light layer of pepper, salt and spice mix. Place the chicken legs on the grid and cook for 35 minutes. Check the internal temperature; chicken is cooked at 62 ° c, but enough fat remains at an internal temperature of 68 ° c;

the texture is therefore better. Remove from grill including let rest for 5 minutes before serving.

Roasted chicken with wild rice and mushrooms

Break with your traditionally roasted chicken and enjoy this variant filled with wild rice, mushrooms and bacon. Guaranteed success!

Calories: 240

fat: 6g

carbs: 20g

protein: 13g

Ingredients

1 whole chicken

1.5 tsp salt

1/2 tsp freshly ground pepper

For the filling

4 tbsp butter

1 chopped onion

200 g bacon cubes

1 cup wild rice

1 cup sliced mushrooms

2 tbsp fresh parsley

salt and pepper to taste

Preparation

1. Start your traeger on 'smoke' with the lid open until you see fire (4 to 5 min.). Set the temperature to 350 ° c and let it heat up for 10 to 15 minutes under the lid closed. Season chicken both in and out with salt and pepper. Melt 2 tbsp butter in a large pan and cook the chopped onion.
2. After 5 minutes add the bacon cubes and fry everything nicely. Stir in the rice and mushrooms as well. Season with salt and pepper. Add 225 cl of water to the mixture and cook under a closed lid until the rice has absorbed all the moisture. Add the parsley.
3. Fill the chicken using the mixture and tie the legs back up with kitchen twine. Place the chicken directly on the grid of your traeger and let it grills for 15 minutes or until you measure a core temperature of about 70 to 75 ° c. Turn frequently. Take chicken out from the grill and allow rest for 10 minutes under foil paper.
4. Serve the sliced chicken with a spoonful of the filling. Tasty!

Chicken breast grill with soya sauce

Calories: 260

fat: 8g

carbs: 37g

protein: 16g

Ingredients

- 750 g chicken breast fillet

For sauce:

- 2 tablespoons soy sauce
- 1 tablespoon honey
- 2 cloves of crushed garlic
- 1 teaspoon of grated fresh ginger
- 1 teaspoon of brown sugar
- 1 tea glass of olive oil
- Salt
- Black pepper

Preparation

1. Take the ingredients for the sauce in a deep bowl and mix.
2. Chop the chicken breast into large pieces. Take the chicken meat into the bowl containing the sauce and mix. Stretch the film and let it rest in the refrigerator for 1 hour. Index of meats in bottles, cook on the grill. Serve hot.

Chicken recipe with sauce

Calories: 245

fat: 11g

carbs: 17g

protein: 26g

Ingredients

- 800 grams of fillet chicken breast
- 2 tablespoons olive oil, 1 tomato
- 1 clove of garlic, 1 small onion bulb
- 1 teaspoon tomato paste
- 1 teaspoon hot sauce (or 1/2 teaspoon powdered red pepper)
- 1 teaspoon of oregano,

- 1 teaspoon of coriander (if desired)
- 1/4 teaspoon cumin

Preparation

1. If you have time to extend the marination period of chicken meat in the sauce mixture you prepare, leave for 1 hour in the refrigerator.
2. You can also cook the chicken with sauce on the grill or pan on greasy paper.
3. Cut the breasts of fillet chicken which you wash in water and dry with paper towel into long thin strips.
4. For the sauce mixture; after peeling the skin, drain the juice of the onion you planed. You can use the posa portion for another meal.
5. Grate the tomato with the thin portion of the grater. Put the onion juice and grated tomatoes in a deep mixing bowl. Mix with olive oil, grated garlic, tomato paste, hot sauce, thyme, cumin and coriander.
6. Take the chopped fillet chicken breasts into the mixing bowl and cover them and leave them in the refrigerator.
7. For long periods of rest (at least one hour and one night if you have time), pass the chicken meat horizontally to the wooden skewers.
8. Cook as soon as possible by inverting the duplex on a pre-heated pan or grill.

9. According to desire; share with your loved ones on heated lavash with the addition of curly lettuce leaves, ring-cut red onions and tomato slices.

Savory chicken thighs with grill marinade

Calories: 211

fat: 4g

carbs: 33g

protein: 28

Ingredients

- One toe garlic (crushed)
- 1/2 tablespoon mustard
- 2 tsp sugar (brown)
- One teaspoon chili powder
- Pepper (black, freshly ground)
- 1 tbsp olive oil
- 5 pcs chicken lower leg

Preparation

1. For the spicy chicken legs with grill marinade, mix the garlic with the mustard, the brown sugar, the chili powder, a pinch of salt and freshly ground pepper. Mix with the oil.
2. Rub in the chicken thighs with the marinade and marinate for 20 minutes.
3. Put the chicken thighs in the basket and push the basket into the pressure cooker. Set the timer to 10-12 minutes.
4. Fry the chicken thighs at 200 ° c until brown. Minimize the temperature to 150 ° c and fry the chicken thighs for another 10 minutes until they are cooked.
5. Serve he spicy chicken leg with barbecue marinade with corn salad and baguette

Organic grilled Italian chicken recipe

Ingredients

- 1 pound of organic chicken breast without bones
- 1/4 cup Italian dressing / marinade

Preparation:

1. Burn your grill over medium heat.
2. If using a grill pan, set the burners to medium heat.
3. Marinate chicken in Italian dressing for at least 1 hour.
4. Spread the chicken breast with Italian dressing / marinade and place on the grill.
5. Boil your chicken and stick it with your Italian dressing / marinade throughout the cooking time.
6. Cook until your chicken reaches the internal temperature of about 20 minutes and turn the chicken halfway to the other side.

California grilled chicken

Ingredients

- 3/4 c. Balsamic vinegar
- 1 teaspoon. Garlic powder
- 2 tbsp. Honey
- 2 tbsp. Extra virgin olive oil
- 2 tsps. Italian spice
- Kosher salt
- Freshly ground black pepper
- 4 boneless chicken breast without skin
- 4 slices of mozzarella
- 4 slices of avocado
- 4 tomato slices
- 2 tbsp. Freshly cut basil for garnish
- Balsamic glaze for drizzling

Preparation

1. In small bowl whisk balsamic vinegar, garlic powder, honey, oil and Italian spices and season with salt and the pepper. Pour the chicken and marinate for 20 minutes.
2. When you are ready to grill, heat the grill to medium high. Grate the oil grills and chicken until charred and cooked through, 8 minutes each side.
3. Top chicken with the mozzarella, avocado and tomato and lid grill melt, 2 minutes.

4. Garnish with basil and then drizzle with some balsamic glaze.

Grilled chicken

Calories: 244

fat: 8g

carbs: 37g

protein: 23g

Ingredients

- 1 whole chicken, dry
- 3 tbsps. Paleo melted cooking fat
- 3 tbsps. Fresh rosemary, finely chopped
- 2 onions, peeled and quartered
- 4 carrots, peeled and cut into slices
- 2 peppers, chopped
- 2 lemons cut in half
- Sea salt and freshly ground black pepper

Preparation

1. Preheat the oven to 204 c.
2. Place the chicken, face down, on a cutting board. Cut along both sides of the spine from one end to the other with kitchen scissors and remove the spine. Turn the chicken breast over and open it like a book. Firmly press the breasts with the palm to flatten them.
3. In a small bowl, mix cooking fat and 2 tablespoons of fat. Of rosemary.
4. Rub the chicken with 2/3 of the fat and rosemary mixture and season the chicken to make it taste with sea salt and ground pepper.
5. Cover a large baking sheet with aluminum foil.
6. Place the chicken right on the baking tray and then surround it with the vegetables and lemons.
7. Pour the mixture of fat and rosemary remaining on the vegetables and season to taste.
8. Put the baking sheet inside the oven for 1 hour or until a meat thermometer indicates 73 c into the thickest part of the breast.
9. Remove the chicken from the oven; squeeze a little lemon juice and go.

Wings recipe with sauce

Calories: 260

fat: 8g

carbs: 37g

protein: 16g

Ingredients

- 1 kilogram chicken wing
- 4 tablespoons sunflower oil
- 4 tablespoons of milk
- 2 tablespoons yogurt
- 1 teaspoon tomato paste
- 1 teaspoon hot sauce
- 2 cloves of garlic
- 1/2 teaspoon of grape vinegar
- 1/2 teaspoon of honey, 1 bay leaf
- 1 teaspoon of oregano
- 1 teaspoon fresh ground black pepper
- 1 teaspoon of salt
- 1 sprig of fresh rosemary

Tip of the winged sauce recipe: extending the marinating mixture will increase the flavor of chicken wings.

Preparation

1. Wash the chicken wings in plenty of water and remove excess water with the help of paper towels.
2. Grate the garlic. Mix sunflower oil, milk, yogurt, tomato paste, hot sauce and honey in a large bowl.
3. Add grated garlic, bay leaf, thyme, freshly ground colored black pepper, extracted rosemary branches and salt. Mix all the ingredients.
4. Put the chicken wings in the sauce mixture you prepared and place them in a single row on the oven tray.
5. Bake into a pre-heated 180 degree oven for 45-50 minutes. Serve hot wings, which draw the sauce and flavored with spices.

Chicken with bbq sauce

Calories: 260

fat: 8g

carbs: 37g

protein: 16g

Ingredients

- 4 pieces of chicken legs
- Salt, pepper
- 300 ml. Bbq sauce or ketchup
- 500 gr. Celery stalk
- 1 tablespoon liquid oil
- Sugar
- 1 dessert spoon vinegar

Preparation

1. Thoroughly wash and clean the chicken thighs, then salt and pepper.
2. Place the thighs on the baking tray with the skins facing down.
3. Bake inside an oven heated to 200 ° for 15 minutes, turn over and cook for another 15 minutes.
4. Spread a thick layer of barbecue sauce or ketchup on them and cook for another 5 minutes.

5. Cut the stems of celery finely, chop the leaves.
6. Celery stalks in oil for 5 minutes, sprinkle with a pinch of sugar sprinkle, circulate vinegar.
7. Add the minced leaves, salt and pepper.
8. Serve the chicken with vegetables and sauce.

Grilled chicken with ranch sauce

Calories: 122

fat: 4g

carbs: 13g

protein: 25g

Ingredients

- Chicken
- 1 lb. Chicken (4 lb.)
- 10 ml (2 teaspoons) salt
- 5 ml (1 teaspoon) of garlic powder
- ½ lemons
- 1 recipe of ranch vinaigrette, salad
- 4 celery stalks, minced
- 1 bulb of fennel, finely chopped
- 1 green onion, chopped
- 30 ml (2 tablespoons) chopped fennel leaves

- 30 ml (2 tablespoons) of olive oil
- 15 ml (1 tablespoon) lemon juice

Preparation

1. On a work surface, using the chef's knife or kitchen scissors, remove the bone from the back of the chicken. Flip the chicken and cut in half in the center of the breasts. Place the pieces in a large glass dish. Sprinkle chicken skin with salt and garlic powder. Rub the outside and then inside of the chicken with the cut part of the lemon. Thoroughly coat with 1/2 cup (125 ml) ranch vinaigrette. Cover and refrigerate 12 hours.
2. Preheat half of the barbecue at high power. Oil the grill on the off side.
3. Drain the meat. Place the chicken on the off-the-grill section, skin side on the grill. Close the barbecue lid. Bake 45 minutes while maintaining a temperature of 200 ° c (400 ° f). Return the chicken and continue cooking for 35 minutes or until a thermometer inserted into the thigh, without letting it touching the bone, indicates 180 ° f (82 ° c) maintaining a temperature of 200 ° c (400 ° f). Finish cooking on the lit section of the barbecue to mark the chicken.

Chicken burgers recipe

Calories: 260

fat: 8g

carbs: 37g

protein: 16g

Ingredients

- 1/2 recipe for chicken nuggets
- 4 hamburgers
- Buns lamb's lettuce
- 200 grams of fries

Ingredients ranch sauce

- 4 tablespoons mayonnaise
- 125 ml buttermilk
- 4 tablespoons low-fat yogurt
- 1 teaspoon dried dill
- 1 teaspoon chives
- Salt and black pepper to taste
- Juice of 1 lime

Preparation

1. Prepare the chicken nuggets as indicated in the recipe, but make them slightly larger so that you have good pieces. Fry the fries.
2. Make the ranch sauce by mixing all the ingredients together well.
3. Cut the hamburger buns open and grill them briefly on the bbq. Use colored bread rolls from brown & serve, which makes it nice and cool. Build up the burger with the lamb's lettuce, chicken nuggets, fries, and the ranch sauce.
4. That's it, enjoy!

Recipe chicken lollipops

Ingredients

- 6 drumsticks
- 4 tablespoons chicken rub
- 2 tablespoons barbecue sauce (optional)
- Extra supplies:
- Barbecue with lid
- Cleaver

Preparation

1. Prepare your barbecue for indirect grilling at a temperature of 160 to 180 degrees.
2. Grab a drumstick and make an indentation 2 inches from the top. You can now push the bottom part down a bit. The top part can now be completely removed - except for the bone. If the last part at the nodule is difficult, this part can also be chopped off. You can cut or cut away the tendons that come out.
3. Put the drumstick down, it's supposed to be upright. If this doesn't work, cut it straight at the bottom as well, until it remains upright. Spread the chicken lollipops generously with the chicken rub.
4. Place the chicken lollipops on the grid and close the lid. As soon as the chicken lollipops have reached a temperature of 70 degrees, you can rub them with barbecue sauce. They are tasty with or without

sauce, so try it out! Then put them back on the grid, close the lid and let them cook until they have reached a temperature of 75 degrees.

Enjoy!

Cuban grilled chicken with salsa fresca

Calories: 260

fat: 8g

carbs: 37g

protein: 16g

Ingredients

- 15 cl of grapefruit juice
- 2 tbsp. Tablespoon olive oil
- 2 tbsp. Coffee garlic granulated
- 2 tbsp. Coffee roasted cumin
- 1 tbsp. Selection hungarian paprika
- 1 tbsp. Coffee chili ground cayenne
- 600 g chicken fillet, cut in half salsa fresca
- 1 grapefruit, peeled raw into quarters
- 80 g of jicama (if not replace with water chestnut or zucchini), diced

- 1 small red onion, minced
- 2 tbsp. Grapefruit juice
- 2 tbsp. Tablespoon olive oil
- 1 tbsp. Chopped fresh cilantro
- 1 tbsp. Chopped fresh jalapeño pepper or ducros cayenne pepper

Preparation

1. For the chicken marinade, pour the grapefruit juice, oil, garlic, cumin, paprika and cayenne pepper in a small bowl and mix well. Place the chicken in a big resalable plastic food bag or in a glass dish.
2. Add the marinade and then mix to coat the chicken pieces well. Refrigerate 30 minutes or longer for the aromas to develop further.
3. Meanwhile, make the salsa by mixing all the ingredients in a small bowl and cover. Keep fresh until ready to serve.
4. Drain the chicken, discard the rest of the marinade. Grill it over fairly high heat 6 to 8 minutes on each side or cook it for 15 to 20 minutes inside an oven preheated to 200 ° c (th. 6/7). Serve it with the salsa fresca.

Asian chicken skewers

Ingredients

- 1/2 cup soy sauce
- 3 tbsp. Orange juice
- 2 tbsp. Of honey
- 1 tbsp. Tablespoon vegetable oil
- 1 tbsp. Sesame oil
- 1 tbsp. Coffee coriander from france
- 1/4 tsp. Coffee garlic granulated
- 1/4 tsp. Coffee ginger
- 500 g chicken breasts in strips

Preparation

1. Combine soy sauce, orange juice, honey, vegetable oil, sesame oil, cilantro, garlic and ginger in a bowl.
2. Place chicken strips inside a large resalable plastic bag or glass dish. Add the marinade and toss to coat them well.
3. Refrigerate 15 minutes or more, for more flavors. Remove the chicken from the marinade. Thread the chicken strips on skewers.
4. Grill on the barbecue over medium-high heat 4 minutes per side or until the chicken is cooked through and golden brown. Serve with fragrant rice or a salad for a lighter dish.

Mexican chicken skewers

Calories: 260

fat: 8g

carbs: 37g

protein: 16g

Ingredients

- 1 kg of chicken breast
- 1 red onion
- 2 red peppers
- 2 green peppers
- 2 plain yogurts
- 1 tbsp. Tablespoons mexican clever mix
- 1 tbsp. Tablespoons paprika hungary
- 1/2 tsp. Coffee chipotle
- 1 tbsp. Tablespoon olive oil
- The juice of a lime
- Guerande sea salt
- Wooden skewers

Preparation

1. In a bowl, prepare marinade: mix the yogurts, lemon juice, olive oil, spices and salt.
2. Cut your chicken breasts into small strips 1 to 2 cm thick. Place them inside a gratin dish and sprinkle them with the marinade. Mix everything well with a spoon and film with cling film. Place the dish in the fridge for 2 to 3 hours.
3. After the marinating time, heat your barbecue. Wash and then cut the peppers into small squares about 3 cm apart. Peel the onion and cut pieces into large squares.
4. Immerse your wooden picks in water for about 5 minutes to prevent them from burning during cooking.
5. Prick a first pan of chicken accordion on a wooden pick, then alternate 2 onions and 2 peppers and close with the second pan of chicken. Close the skewers on both sides with a pepper and an onion and arrange them in a presentation dish.
6. Heat your barbecue. Place your skewers on the grill and then cook them for about ten minutes on each side until they are well grilled.

Oriental chicken drumsticks

Ingredients

- 12 chicken drumsticks
- 2 tbsp. Soup clever blend eastern
- 2 tbsp. Tablespoon olive oil
- 1 knob of butter

Preparation

1. Brown the chicken drumsticks (3 per person) in a little oil and a knob of butter for 20 min. Turning them over very often.
2. At the end of cooking, salt and sprinkle with 2 tbsp. Oriental clever mix. Stop cooking.

Trick

Oriental chicken drumsticks can be enjoyed hot, as an aperitif or as a main course with a green salad or sautéed vegetables.

Tandoori chicken with grilled spices

Ingredients

- 2 tbsp. Cook art toasted spice mix for tandoori ducros
- 1/2 tsp. Coffee fresh mint or mint ducros
- 1 tbsp. Coffee ground coriander
- 100 g greek yogurt
- 2 tbsp. Tablespoon vegetable oil
- 4 beautiful chicken breasts

Preparation

1. Inside a bowl, prepare the marinade by mixing the herbs, cook art spice blend, yogurt, lemon juice and oil.
2. Cut each chicken breast 4 times with a sharp knife and place them in the marinade. Coat them well.
3. Cover and then let sit in the fridge for at least 30 minutes (or overnight for an even tastier result).
4. Preheat the grill at medium heat or prepare your barbecue.
5. Cook the marinated chicken breasts on a grill for 20 to 25 minutes, turning them regularly. The escaping cooking juices should be clear and the surface lightly browned.
6. Check the doneness and serve very hot.

CHAPTER 8

FISH AND SEAFOOD RECIPES

Small grilled red mullet with seaweed

Calories: 260

fat: 8g

carbs: 37g

protein: 16g

Ingredients

- 12 small red mullet
- 1 tbsp. Rosemary coffee
- 1 handful of flat seaweed sold at the fishmonger's
- 1 tbsp. Tablespoon olive oil
- 2 yellow lemons
- 1 5 berry grinder - sweet

Preparation

1. Have the red mullet drained by the fishmonger. Salt and turn the mill 5 berries inside and out, then sprinkle with rosemary.
2. Wrap each of them in a large sheet of seaweed, making it adhere well. Then brush the turbaned red mullet with olive oil.
3. Grill on a barbecue with hot embers, without flames, about 6 min on each side. Serve with lemons.

Cajun marinated salmon fillets

Ingredients

- 4 salmon fillets of 150 to 175g each
- 1 sachet cajun bbq mix
- 2 tbsp. Tablespoon olive oil
- 1 lemon juice

Preparation

1. Wipe the salmon fillets with a paper towel.
2. Mix all the other ingredients together and coat the salmon fillets in a deep dish. Let stand in the fridge for 15-20 minutes.
3. Bake on the barbecue or grill for 10 to 20 minutes.

Tuna skewer with spicy sauce

Ingredients

- 2 nice slices of tuna
- 2 courgettes
- 1 lemon juice
- 1 tbsp. Coffee onion première flavor
- 2 pinch ground cayenne pepper
- 3 tbsp. Tablespoon olive oil

Preparation

1. Cut the tuna slices into cubes. Do the same with the zucchini after washing them. Place them in a deep dish and pour in the lemon juice, olive oil, chili and onion. Mix well.
2. Cover the dish and let stand in the fridge for at least an hour. At the end of this time, prick the pieces of tuna and zucchini, alternating them on skewers.
3. Cook on the grill or on a plancha for a few minutes, turning regularly so that the pieces are golden brown;
4. Serve with basmati rice.

Grilled asparagus with fish

Seasonal dish with asparagus

Calories: 280

Fat: 12.5g

Sodium: 86mg

Carbohydrates: 0g

Protein: 39.2g

Ingredients

- 4 to 5 thick, white asparagus per person (5 to 6 green asparagus per person)
- Fresh farmer's butter (+/- 1 tablespoon per person) for the asparagus
- +/- 150 to 200 gr for the fish (or oil)
- Parsley
- Possibly capers or caper apple
- Nutmeg, pepper & salt
- Preferably take white & a relatively firm fish (such as tail fish, whiting - or alternatively sole, halibut, cod or ray wing)
- Aluminum foil
- Aluminum containers for cooking butter & asparagus (semi-cooked will then be grilled briefly)

Preparation

1. Heat the traeger to maximum.
2. Peel the asparagus and remove the hard wood part from the stem.
3. Place an aluminum container with the white butter and some water in the traeger, let it get hot. Place the asparagus in the aluminum dish and season with a little coarse pepper, salt and nutmeg and cover with the aluminum foil. Leave to poach for 10 to 20 minutes.
4. Meanwhile, season the fish melt the butter in an aluminum dish. Grill the fish very briefly and place in the aluminum dish, baste it with the butter and garnish with the capers or the caper apple.
5. Remove the asparagus from the traeger, check whether they are just tender enough (slightly harder than al dente) and grill them briefly (only for the caramelized color)
6. Arrange the fish on a plate, drizzle some cooking oil / gravy over the fish with some capers. Place the asparagus alongside the fish and / or cut diagonally (more decorative) and arrange them on the plate.
7. Finish with parsley and season more if necessary.

Tasty!

Bbq oysters

Calories: 244

fat: 8g

carbs: 37g

protein: 23g

Ingredients

- 12 esters (1pp)
- Spring onion cut into fine rings (only the green part)
- Traeger "sweet & heat" bbq sauce
- Breadcrumbs
- Hard grated cheese
- 250gr herb butter

Preparation

1. A preheated traeger at +/- 190 ° c.
2. Open the esters and remove the excess juice. Garnish the esters with some breadcrumbs and place in the traeger for +/- 5 minutes.
3. Open the traeger and place a spoon / slice of herb butter on each oyster. Let it cook for like 5 to 7 minutes.
4. Finish with some traeger "sweet & heat" bbq sauce in slow onion and let it cool for +/- 5 minutes.

Tasty!

Mussels with green onions and ginger

Calories: 244

fat: 8g

carbs: 37g

protein: 23g

Ingredients

- 2 tables. L. - olive oil
- 1 table. L. - chopped ginger
- 3-4 pcs. - a clove of garlic
- 1 pc. - chili peppers
- 2 bunches - green onions
- ½ glass - dry white wine
- 20 pcs. - peeled mussels
- 4 tables. L. – butter
- To taste - salt.

Preparation

1. Preheat the grill to a medium temperature of 110 degrees.

2. Pour olive oil into container, put butter. Once the oil is hot enough, put chopped garlic, and finely chopped hot peppers, ginger root and half a green onion.

3. Cook for no more than 1 minute.

4. Add mussels, pour in wine (can be replaced with water), stir quickly.

5. Cook it with the lid closed for 5 minutes (stirring occasionally). The mussels are ready when they open.

6. Salt is added at the end part of the cooking.

7. Transfer the hot seafood to a dish, sprinkle with the remaining onions on top.

It is better to serve seafood with bread, which can also be fried on the grill with the addition of butter (one minute on each side). Any kind of rice or vegetables can be used as a supplement. If you like spices, feel free to add according to your taste.

Grilled shrimps in aromatic marinade

Calories: 280

Fat: 12.5g

Sodium: 86mg

Protein: 39.2g

Ingredients

- 800 g - peeled shrimp
- 1 table. L. - olive oil
- 3 tables. L. - melted butter
- 6 cloves – garlic
- 2 tables. L. – honey
- 2 tables. L. - lime juice
- 1/2 tea l. – salt
- To taste - ground red and black pepper.

Preparation

1. Mix butter with olive oil. Add lime juice, honey, and minced garlic.
2. Separately mix salt, black and red pepper. Spicy herbs can be added if desired.
3. Sprinkle the shrimp with the dry mixture, stir. Then let sit for 15 minutes.

4. Pour the cooked marinade over, then string on wooden sticks or skewers.
5. Preheat the grill to 160 degrees. Place the seafood on the wire rack.
6. Cook each side for 3 minutes. The shrimp are well cooked when they turn transparent.
7. Serve hot to the table.

It is important not to overexpose the grilled shrimp. Otherwise they will become hard.

Grilled seafood salad and salsa verde with Thai basil

Ingredients

- Salsa verde
- 30 g (1 cup) Thai basil leaves
- 30 g (1 cup) coriander leaves
- 1/4 cup (60 ml) vegetable oil
- 45 ml (3 tablespoons) lime juice
- 30 ml (2 tablespoons) of water
- 1 green onion, cut into sections
- Seafood and vegetables
- 900 g (2 lb) of mussels, cleaned
- 225 g (1/2 lb) medium shrimp (31-40), shelled and deveined

- 4 small squid, trimmed
- 15 ml (1 tablespoon) vegetable oil
- 15 ml (1 tablespoon) lime juice
- 10 ml (2 teaspoons) fish sauce
- 2 teaspoons (10 ml) turmeric
- 1 bulb of fennel, thinly sliced with mandolin
- 400 g (2 cups) baby potatoes, cooked
- 2 green onions, chopped
- 1 tomato, quartered
- Thai basil leaves, to taste

Preparation

1. Salsa verde
2. In the food processor, finely grind all the ingredients.
3. Seafood and vegetables
4. Preheat the barbecue to high power. Oil the grill.
5. In a large bowl, combine mussels, shrimp, squid, oil, lime juice, fish sauce and turmeric. Salt and pepper.
6. Place the mussels directly on the barbecue grill. Close the barbecue lid and cook the mussels for 3 to 5 minutes or until they are all open. Discard those that remain closed. Place in a bowl. Shell the mussels (keep some for service, if desired).
7. Grill shrimp and squid for 2 to 3 minutes per side or until shrimp and squid are cooked and browned. On a work surface, cut squid into 1 cm (1/2 inch) slices.

8. Place the fennel in a bowl. Lightly oil, season with salt and pepper.
9. Spread seafood and vegetables on plates. Sprinkle salsa verde and garnish with Thai basil leaves.

Grilled shrimp with mint sauce

Calories: 250

Fat: 11g

Protein: 39.2g

Ingredients

- 500 g shrimp
- Half of fresh mint
- 1 - 2 shallots
- 3 cloves of garlic
- 2 tablespoons apple cider vinegar
- 1 tea glass of olive oil
- 1 teaspoon of sugar
- 2 teaspoons of salt
- 1 teaspoon of red paprika

Preparation

1. For the sauce, put all ingredients except olive oil into the blender and run the blender.
2. Slowly add olive oil and have a thick consistency. Extract the shrimps and put them in a deep dish. Hover over the sauce and find all sides.
3. Wrap the stretch film and leave in the refrigerator for at least 2-3 hours. Pass the prawns to the bottle.
4. Cook on overheated grill. Serve hot.

Grilled sea bass with vegetables

Ingredients

- 2 perch
- 1 onion
- 2 cloves of garlic
- 1 potato
- 1 carrot
- 1 lemon
- 2 sprigs of rosemary
- 1 tea glass of olive oil
- 2 cloves of crushed garlic
- 1 teaspoon red ground pepper
- 1 teaspoon of red paprika
- 1 teaspoon black pepper
- 2 teaspoons of salt

Preparation

1. Clean the perch. Slice all vegetables to be very thin. You filled the fish with vegetables.
2. Add the rosemary. Mix the ingredients for the sauce thoroughly with a fork.
3. Tie the fish with the rope and take them to the barbecue.
4. Brush with the help of the sauce you prepare and cook the fish duplex. Serve.

Smoked ham

Ingredients

- 1.6 kilograms (2.7 kilograms) "ready to eat" ham
- 1 cup (240 milliliters) of pineapple juice
- 3/4 cup (180 milliliters) chicken stock
- 1/2 cup (120 milliliters) honey
- 2 tablespoons (30 milliliters) of vegetable oil
- 1 tablespoon (15 milliliters) of black pepper
- 1 tablespoon (15 milliliters) red pepper
- 1 tablespoon (15 milliliters) sugar
- 2 teaspoons (10 milliliters) of salt
- 2 teaspoons (10 milliliters) of dry mustard
- 1/2 teaspoon (2.5 milliliters) of cayenne
- 1/2 teaspoon (2.5 milliliters)
- Carnations

Preparation

1. The night before smoking, mix pepper, paprika, sugar, salt, 1 teaspoon of dry mustard and cayenne. Spread on the surface of the dough, wrap in foil and refrigerate overnight.
2. In the morning, take the ham out of the refrigerator and let it sit for 1 hour. Remove the foil. Meanwhile the smoker prepares. You will be smoking like 210 degrees f / 100 degrees c for 6 hours.
3. Mix 3/4 cup (180 milliliters) of chicken stock, pineapple juice, vegetable oil, 1/2 teaspoon (2.5

milliliters) of dry mustard and cloves. Heat over medium heat until completely mixed.
4. Put the bath on the cigarette and put it on the plate with the sauce every hour. While smoking in the dough, it is prepared by mixing honey, 1/4 cup (60 milliliters), pineapple juice, 1/2 teaspoon (2.5 milliliters) dry mustard and a mixture of grass cloves. In the last hour of smoking, generously brush several times with glaze.

Grilled lobster tails

Ingredients

- 6 lobster tails
- 1/4 cup / 60 ml
- Olive oil or melted butter
- 1/4 cup or 60 ml of lemon juice
- 1 tablespoon / 15 ml fresh dill
- 1 teaspoon / 5 ml salt

Preparation

1. Preheat grill for medium-high heat.
2. Cut the lobster tails lengthwise in half the meat. Pat dry with a paper towel
3. Combine remaining part of the ingredients in small mixing bowl until salt dissolves. Liberally, brush mix on the flesh of lobster tails.

4. Place the lobster inside the grill and cook for 5-7 minutes depending on the size of the lobster tail, longer cooking may be required.
5. Make sure you turn once during the cooking process. Lobster tails will be made when the internal temperature of the meat reaches 140 degrees f.
6. Take it from the fire and serve. Prepare a double mustard butter mixture and set the halves apart to serve the dipping sauce for grilled lobster.

Rib-eye smoked as a whole with smoked aubergines

Calories: 280

Fat: 12.5g

Sodium: 86mg

Carbohydrates: 0g

Protein: 39.2g

Ingredients

- 1 rib eye (roast beef, approx. 2 kg)
- Sea salt (coarse)
- Pepper (good, of your choice)
- 4 tbsp. Adis beef rub
- 4 tbsps. Olive oil
- 300 ml apple juice
- 2 aubergines
- 100 g onions (red, finely chopped)
- 1 bunch of chives (finely chopped)
- 100 g olives (finely chopped)
- Salt
- Pepper
- 1/2 lemon (lemon juice)
- 4 tbsp. Olive oil

Preparation

1. For the rib-eye smoked as a whole, first salt and pepper the rib-eye. You can do this a few hours before the barbecue or the evening before.
2. Then place on a smoker (pellet smoker, water smoker or locomotive) and smoke at 120 ° c to a core temperature of 56 ° c. It is important to mop or brush the rib eye more often.
3. take the apple juice, boil it and mix in 4 tablespoons of adis beef rub, boil the juice into a creamy sauce and mop the rib eye with it again and again.
4. With the water smoker it is recommended to work with wood chips in order to get a nice smoke aroma (less is more), with the pellet smoker the smoke aromas arise by themselves, this is the grill for "lazy and intelligent people".
5. With the locomotive you have to be careful with the wood. In order to avoid a sharp smoke, the wood must be debarked and the heat and air supply must be precisely regulated - this is a preparation method for freaks and barbecues in its perfection.
6. The constant temperature of 120 ° c and the mopping with the marinade creates a wonderful crust.
7. Halve the aubergine lengthways, cut into the inside with a small sharp knife and then cut across to create a cubic pattern; the shell should not be damaged.
8. Smoke for 35-40 minutes, softening the pulp; pour the chopped onions, chives, olives, lemon juice and

olive oil over them and let them smoke. The soft pulp can then be wonderfully spooned out.
9. Serve the rib eye with smoked aubergines.

Tips

This dish can be prepared on different grills, although the grilling time can vary considerably.

You can also grill the rib eye all around and only then smoke it; in order to get less smoke aromas, wrap the grilled food in aluminum foil while smoking.

Smoked turkey leg

Ingredients

Servings: 6

- 1 turkey legs (2 1/2 kg)
- 4 tbsps. Rub (spice mix for poultry)

Preparation

1. For the smoked turkey leg, first wash the turkey leg, pat dry and rub generously with the spice mixture.
2. Wrap in cling film or covered in the refrigerator for 24 hours.
3. The turkey leg is provided with a meat thermometer and reached at about 160 ° c until a core temperature of 80 ° c, burn incense in smoker or on the gas or kettle grill.

Organic beef pastrami

Calories: 280

Fat: 12.5g

Sodium: 86mg

Carbohydrates: 0g

Protein: 39.2g

Ingredients

Servings: 10

For the spice:

- 30 g pepper (ground)
- 60 g herbs (provence)
- 40 g herbs (wild, mixed, dried, e.g. Wild garlic, elderflower, nettle, black clover, watercress, thyme)
- 160 g sugar (brown)
- 100 g paprika powder
- 350 g sea salt (coarse)
- 60 g garlic powder
- 5 g chili flakes for the pastrami:
- 2000 g beef (organic beef rump or nuts)
- 100 g hickory chips (or beech chips, soaked for at least 30 minutes, for smoking)

For the mustard butter:

- 120 g butter
- 40 g dijon mustard
- Salt
- Pepper

Also:

- 20 slice (s) of country bread
- 50 g rocket

Preparation

1. For the organic beef pastrami, first weigh and mix all the ingredients for the spice.
2. The meats prepare. To do this, pat the meat dry and rub the spice all around. Wrap in baking paper and then in cling film and leave to marinate for at least 24 hours, preferably 48 hours.
3. Prepare the smoker or the kettle grill for grilling. With the smoker you can use the minion principle for the arrangement of the briquettes, with the kettle grill prepare the grill with around 8 briquettes per side, reheating is necessary! Fill the water bowl of the smoker or, for the kettle grill, place a water bowl between the fire baskets; a water bowl is also placed in the grill for the gas grill.
4. For the mustard butter, beat the butter until foamy white, mix in the mustard, season with salt and pepper.

5. For the pastrami, position a core thermometer in the middle of the meat, place the meat on the clean grate, close the lid and close the ventilation slide a third to a maximum of half. ⅓ put the smoking chips directly into the embers and repeat every 30 minutes. Smoke until a core temperature of 60 ° c is reached (3-4 hours at 100 ° c), then let it cool for 20 minutes, and then cut into fine slices.
6. Cut the country bread into slices and brush with the mustard butter. Spread some rocket on top and top with the organic beef pastrami.

Tips

The pastrami from organic beef is grilled on indirect heat, which is possible on both the smoker and the kettle grill. Only on the gas grill is it more difficult to keep the temperature so low (this is only possible with very large grills).

Ikan panggang (Indonesian grilled fish)

Calories: 280

Fat: 12.5g

Sodium: 86mg

Carbohydrates: 0g

Protein: 39.2g

Ingredients

- 4 whole mackerel emptied
- 2 cardamom seeds
- 2 whole cayenne pepper, finely chopped
- 1 tbsp. Coffee ginger
- 3 mill towers camargue salt mill
- 2 tbsp. Soup
- 2 tbsp. Soup lemongrass
- 1 tbsp. Coffee turmeric
- 2 limes
- 20 cl of coconut cream

Preparation

1. Extract the cardamom seeds from their pod and coarsely pound them in a mortar
2. Add the chili, ginger and salt and grind the mixture. Transfer to a container, then stir in the shallot, lemongrass and turmeric. Mix.
3. Cut the limes in half. Extract the flesh with a spoon, then dice it and add it to the mixture. Add the coconut cream and mix.
4. Cut 3 slits diagonally on each side of the mackerel going up to the dorsal ridge to allow the marinade to soak up the flesh of the fish.
5. Brush the mackerel with the marinade. Covers it up and let sit in the refrigerator for 30 minutes.
6. Preheat the grill. Cook the mackerel, 4 to 5 minutes per side, basting frequently, until golden brown and cooked through. Decorate with lime wedges and serve immediately.

Tips

You can make this dish by replacing the mackerel with another fish, such as sea bream.

CHAPTER 9

GAME RECIPES

Game meat racks

Calories: 150

Fat: 15g

Protein: 29.2g

Ingredients

- 500 g of game minced meat (leg, shoulder of stag or roe deer)
- 100 ml milk (lukewarm)
- 100 g bacon cubes
- 1 teaspoon mustard (medium hot)
- 3 shallots
- 2 cloves of garlic
- 2 juniper berries
- 2 sprig (s) of thyme
- 2 sprig (s) of rosemary
- 1 roll (from the day before)
- 1 egg
- Salt
- Pepper

- Rapeseed oil

Preparation

1. Debark the bread and dice it. Pour the milk over it and allow it steep for 10 minutes.
2. Peel and chop the shallots and garlic.
3. Sweat the bacon, shallots and garlic in 1 tablespoon of rapeseed oil, allow cooling a little. Finely grind the juniper berries. Pluck the thyme and rosemary and chop finely.
4. Mix the minced meat with the roll, bacon mixture, juniper berries, mustard, egg and the herbs and season with salt and pepper.
5. Shape the mixture into 8 even labels and cover them in the refrigerator for about 1 hour.
6. Prepare grill for direct and indirect heat (200 ° c). If a charcoal grill (57) is used, you need a 2/3 full chimney with glowed briquettes.
7. Spray the hot grate with anti-stick spray and grill the labels directly on both sides for 2-3 minutes. Then position it indirectly and continue grilling until a core temperature of 65 ° c is reached.

All American bbq spare ribs

When the ribs are too plain, season them firmly to stimulate your guests' appetites. Do says for your next block party.

Ingredients

- 2 racks of grill, 2.75 kg of skinned pork ribs
- 2 to 3 tbsp chicken seasoning
- 1 cup of apple juice, cider or beer
- 50 g barbecue sauce

Preparation

1. Remove the silver skin part on the back of the ribs.
2. Sprinkle the chicken seasoning on both sides of the ribs. When you are ready to cook, start the traeger grill on smoke with the lid open until there is a good fire (4 to 5 minutes).
3. Increase the temperature to 95 ° c and preheat with the lid closed for 10 to 15 minutes. Arrange the ribs on the racks or grid, with the bones down. Cook for 3 to 4 hours. After 1 hour, spray with call juice. Repeat said after every hour of cooking. After 3 to 4 hours of cooking, rub the ribs with the barbecue sauce. Grill for another 30 minutes to 1 hour, cut into individual ribs and serve with extra barbecue sauce.

Wild boar t-bone steak with red cabbage quinoa pan

T-bone or tomahawk steak - the "new cuts" are on everyone's lips. We tested the wild variety - certainly not as big as a beef steak - but delicious, regional and sustainable!

Preparation

1. The t-bone steak is obtained by a cross section in the back part and consists of back and loin. The "t" - shaped lumbar vertebra is eponymous. To cut the steak out of a boar, the waiting animal is split once along the spine. The clubs are triggered; the back sawed at the level of the loin in three to four centimeters thick steaks. Remove those silver skin on the back side.

2. Season the steaks with oil, salt, smoked paprika and a little sugar. Now rest for 30 minutes.

3. Rinse the quinoa seeds under running water and drain. Cut the onions and boar bacon into thin strips and fry in a little oil in the oven. Now add the seeds, also roast briefly, with juice of an orange and wildfond deglaze. Add the sliced red cabbage, apple and carrots, salt and sugar, cover and simmer for about 60 minutes. Occasionally stir and pour in the stock. At the end of the cooking, the liquid should have been absorbed by the quinoa seeds as much as possible. Season again with salt and pepper.

4. The steaks only need ten to twelve minutes and can reach the grill just before the end of the cooking time of the quinoa pan. Grill at high temperature and turn several times.

5. Put quinoa and vegetables on a plate and refine with fresh tomatoes, leeks, chopped hazelnut kernels and feta cheese. Then serve the steaks. Season with pepper.

Venison on the salmon board - brown trout from the embers

Preparation

1. Stoke up a fire and prepare a large ember bed. Help with charcoal.

2. Remove the venison from the silver skin; rub with olive oil and salt. Oil the salmon board as well. Spread plenty of thyme, sage, rosemary and other herbs on the salmon board as you like. Place the back on it and fasten it with the clasp.

3. Place the salmon board so close to the fire that it is easy to stand for ten seconds with your hand. After about 60 minutes, turn your back and cook for another 20 to 30 minutes on the fire. Whether the meat is cooked is best checked with a roasting thermometer. At 53 degrees celsius core temperature, the meat is tender pink.

4. Remove brown trout, rinse off and dab dry. Salt and sugar from inside and outside. Quarter the cherry tomatoes, season with a little salt, coconut sugar and tomato vinegar and add a handful of Bromberg berries. Put the mass in the abdominal cavity of the trout.

5. Pick big leaves from the sorrel, spread them slightly overlapping and wrap the fish in them. Just before the venison is ready, put the trout in the

direct embers and cover them. Cook for ten minutes.

6. Also place vegetables in direct embers until the skin is slightly charred. Remove; peel off the skin, cut small and season with olive oil, salt and pepper. Remove the venison from the bone and cut into medallions, salt again and pepper. Strain the trout from the sorrel and serve with vegetables and venison.

Side to the bone with pepper and rosemary

Ingredients

- 2 large ribs with beef bone
- 6 sprigs of fresh rosemary
- Coarse salt
- Big pepper and pepper

Preparation

1. Add salt including pepper both sides of the pieces of meat.
2. Let stand 10 minutes.
3. Brush the meat with the olive oil.
4. Marinate 5 minutes.
5. Cook ribs to bone on the barbecue 2-3 minutes per side.

6. Serve hot with large pepper and rosemary.

Grilled mallard duck breast on crunchy vegetables

Description

Does not grill, does not exist... Venison does not just mean braise or cook for a long time. The mallard duck breasts are prepared on the griddle in a few minutes and served together with the vegetables. Probably the one who still has some in the freezer.

Preparation

1. The marinade: mix orange with a dash of olive oil and the juice of an orange. Pluck and chop thyme and rosemary leaves, peel and grate a thumb-sized piece of ginger, crush the garlic clove and add to the oil-juice mixture with the chili flakes and the honey. Now season with salt and pepper.

2. Wash the mallard ducks, pat dry and marinate in the fridge for about two hours. Then remove from the marinade and scrape off the residue with a knife.

3. For the supplement, wash mangetout and paprika. Cut those peppers into strips, onions into rings. Sprinkle a little oil in a fire-proof pans and sauté. Season with salt, pepper and a little sugar.

4. Now grill the mallard ducks in direct heat for about six minutes per side.

5. Serving: cut open the baguette. Pour vegetables and oil over the baguette, cut the duck breast and place it on top. Season it again with a little pepper and salt. The crispy baguette with crispy vegetables and tender mallard duck is ready.

Recipe spare ribs

Ingredients

- 1500 grams spareribs
- 2 tablespoons mustard
- 3 tablespoons mother of all rubs
- 4 tablespoons cola bbq sauce
- 25 grams butter

Preparation

1. Rinse the ribs well, pat them dry and remove the fleece. Make sure you use a handy knife for this (no sharp point). Make an opening by sliding the knife between the fleeces and carefully unravel the fleece.
2. Use your fingers for this, but you can also use the knife. Make sure you don't damage the meat itself by running your knife only along the bone (and not along the meat).

3. Cut off loose pieces of meat and fat at the top and cut the ribs in half.
4. Coat the bottom with mustard and sprinkle with half of the rub. Flip the ribs and grease the top with mustard as well and sprinkle with the other half of the rub.
5. Prepare the bbq for indirect grilling at a temperature of 110 degrees. Add the smoking wood to the coals as soon as the bbq is up to temperature.
6. Place the ribs on the bbq (the indirect part) and smoke the ribs for about an hour.
7. Place the ribs all in a separate aluminum container, add a small knob of butter and wrap the containers tightly with aluminum foil so that no more air can reach.
8. Place the ribs in the trays on the bbq for another two hours.
9. Remove the ribs from the containers and place them on the wire rack on the indirect part for another 20 minutes and brush the ribs with barbecue sauce.
10. Ready and enjoy!

Tips

For anyone who prefers not to eat pork, you can also replace the spare ribs with veal spare ribs. These are slightly less fat, but also have a very tasty taste.

Fried poultry or game with garnish

Ingredients

- 250 g chicken, or 250 g turkey, or 1/4 pheasant, 2/3 hazel grouse or gray partridge
- 6 g butter
- 25 g mayonnaise with gherkins
- Lettuce leaves or parsley (for garnish) (optional)
- 150 g ready-made garnish of green lettuce leaves, pickled cucumbers, red cabbage, provencal cabbage, pickled tomatoes, pickled apples and pears
- Salt

Preparation

1. Chilled fried poultry is cut into portions. Hazel grouse and partridge are used whole or carcasses are cut in half (see the materials "features of frying poultry and game" and "refueling of poultry and game").
2. Pieces of poultry or game are placed on a dish, garnished with bouquets of green lettuce, pickled cucumbers, red cabbage, provencal cabbage, pickled tomatoes, as well as pickled pears and apples
3. On top, the dish is additionally decorated with salad leaves or parsley sprigs. Separately, mayonnaise with gherkins is served in a gravy boat (see "sauce mayonnaise with gherkins").

Guinea fowl stuffed with vegetables

Ingredients

- 1 guinea fowl
- 2 shallots
- 13 cloves of garlic
- 20 g parsley
- Salt
- Olive oil
- 10 onions cut into quarters
- 5 large potatoes cut into quarters
- 3 pickled tomatoes
- 4 fresh or canned tomatoes (skinless and cut into quarters)
- Fresh thyme
- 200 g chicken broth or broth from any other poultry
- 20-30 g butter
- Ground black pepper

Preparation

1. Stuff the guinea fowl with 2 shallots, 3 cloves of garlic, a slice of butter, thyme and chopped parsley. Outside, pepper and salt the guinea fowl.
2. Put the stuffed guinea fowl in a cast-iron roaster and fry on all sides in a large amount of olive oil. After that, take out the guinea fowl and put it aside temporarily, and fry the potatoes, onions and garlic cloves in olive oil. Add chopped tomatoes (both) to vegetables. Put thyme, salt and ground pepper here.

Pour in 100 g of broth. Place the guinea fowl on a layer of vegetables.
3. Place the roaster in an oven preheated to 170 degrees. Keep the guinea fowl there for 75 minutes. Moreover, every 15 minutes it is necessary to water the guinea fowl from above with the remaining broth.

Partridge with cabbage

Ingredients

- 1 kg of white cabbage (1 small head of cabbage)
- 2 partridges
- 200 g tea sausage
- 15 g smoked brisket
- 50 g butter
- 2 carrots
- 2 onions
- 2 carnation buds
- Salt
- Ground black pepper
- 15 g parsley
- Water

Preparation

1. Cut the head of cabbage in 4 parts. Remove the stump and thick ribs. Then immerse the cabbage in boiling salted water for 2 minutes. Then remove the cabbage from the boiling water, rinse with cold

water, place the cabbage in a colander and let the water drain.
2. Brown the partridges in oil in a frying pan, then salt and pepper.
3. Put chopped cabbage and carrots, sprigs of greens, as well as 2 onions in a pressure cooker (or a rooster), in each of which first stick 1 clove bud. After that, pour 125 g of boiling water into a pressure cooker, add salt and pepper. Bring out the contents of the cooker to a boil with the lid open.
4. Place the sautéed partridge pieces in a pressure cooker. Add finely chopped sausage and brisket there. Close the pressure cooker (or goose maker) with a lid and simmer the partridges in the pressure cooker for 30 minutes, and in the goose maker for 1 hour.

Quail on the grill marinated with vinegar and onions

Ingredients

- Onions - 2 pcs.
- Vinegar (9%) - 30 ml
- Salt to taste
- Ground black pepper - to taste
- Garlic - 1 clove.

Preparation

1. Wash quail carcasses under running cold water, dry on paper towels and put on a cutting board with the backup.
2. Using kitchen scissors, cut each quail along the back, unfold the ribs to the sides and lay the carcass breast up. Beat the carcass lightly with a meat hammer (you can use the handle of a knife instead of a hammer).
3. For the marinade, peel and cut onions into several pieces. Fold in a blender and puree with a clove of garlic.
4. In a separate bowl, mix the vinegar with 50 ml of cold water.
5. Place the quail carcasses in a suitable bowl or food container, shifting with onion and garlic gruel, sprinkle with salt and pepper to taste. Stir it well so

that the meat is well covered with the onion mass on all sides.
6. Pour diluted vinegar over the quail, stir, put a little oppression and put in the refrigerator for 2-3 hours, or better overnight.
7. Burn firewood in the grill to the "gray" coals. Grease the sieve with vegetable oil, lay the quail carcasses, laying them out, as shown in the photo. Remember to shake off all the onions from them.
8. Bake over glowing coals, turning the wire rack from one side to the other from time to time. The quails on the wire rack are ready in about 20 minutes. Their readiness can be easily checked by piercing the breast with a knife: if clear juice flows out without impurities of blood, then the meat can be removed from the barbecue. Transfer the finished quails to a dish, cover with foil and let them rest for another 20 minutes. Then you can serve it with fresh vegetables, herbs and sauce to taste. Enjoy your meal!

Filet mignon with Bernese sauce

Bernese sauce perfectly highlights the flavor of the filet mignon. It is a very rich, elegant and sophisticated dish that you can prepare for a special occasion. Cook the meat with the term you like the most so that each bite is an unforgettable experience.

Ingredients

- 4 servings
- 1/3 cup white vinegar
- 1/3 cup dry white wine
- 1 teaspoon of pepper
- 1 teaspoon minced shallot
- 2 teaspoons chopped parsley
- 1/4 of teaspoon of tarragon
- 3 pieces of egg yolk
- 4 pieces of beef fillet 2 cm thick
- 1 pinch of salt

Preparation

1. Combine wine, vinegar, pepper, shallots and tarragon, heat and reduce to have 1/3 cup. Strain it and reserve.
2. Put a bowl on a water bath, the yolks and the vinegar mixture and heat moving with a balloon whisk to begin to thicken, then put the parsley and remove from heat immediately and set aside.
3. Heat the grill and when it is very hot put a little oil and seal the fillets on the 2 sides, to brown a little and put salt and pepper.

4. Once the steaks are well cooked. Serve immediately with the Bernese sauce.

Tasty bbq ribs

This recipe is a delicious dish of tasty bbq ribs so you can prepare your whole family as a main course. Accompany with a delicious salad and surprise them with these new flavors.

Ingredients

- 8 servings
- 2 ribs racks of ribs
- 2 1/2 teaspoons brown sugars
- 1 1/4 teaspoons instant coffees
- 1 1/4 teaspoons kosher salt
- 1 1/4 teaspoons garlic powder
- 1 1/4 teaspoons coriander laces
- 3/4 teaspoon ground black pepper extra special
- 1/4 of teaspoon of cocoa powder
- 1 teaspoon vegetable oil
- 1 1/2 cups dry red wine
- 2 tablespoons canola oil
- 2 tablespoons chopped white onion
- 2 cups of catsup sauce
- 1 1/2 cups apple cider vinegar
- 3/4 cup brown sugar

- 1 1/2 tablespoons of chicken broth
- 3 tablespoons dijon mustard
- 2 teaspoons chili powder
- 2 teaspoons marinated chipotle chili sauce

Preparation

For the ribs:

1. Arrange the racks of ribs on a baking sheet with edges or inside a large roasting pan.
2. Using a knife, remove the membranes from the bone side of the ribs (this step is very important to make the ribs tender).
3. Dry the ribs with a paper towel; place on the grill with the meat side facing up.
4. Combine the sugar, coffee granules, salt, garlic powder, coriander, pepper and cocoa in the spice grinder; cover and process until smooth.
5. Lightly rub the ribs with oil.
6. Sprinkle with the mixture, pressing it gently to assist it adhere to the ribs.
7. Let stand at room temperature for not more than 1 hour.
8. Preheat oven to 250 f. Pour the beer into the bottom of the baking sheet.
9. Cover the bowl with foil, bake for 4 to 5 hours (this will be enough to make the meat tender, but it won't fall off the bones).
10. Prepare the bbq sauce during the last 30 minutes of baking.

11. Preheat the grill.
12. Grill the ribs over medium heat, turning once, for 5 minutes. Spread with sauce during roasting. Let the ribs stand for like 10 minutes before serving.

For bbq sauce:

1. Heat the oil inside a medium saucepan over medium heat.
2. Add onion, and then cook for 3 minutes or until tender.
3. Add the catsup sauce, vinegar, sugar and broth. Stir until the sugar and the broth dissolve.
4. Add mustard, chili powder and marinade. Cover and cook for 30 minutes. The sauce will thicken as it simmers.

CHAPTER 10

VEGETABLE RECIPES

Stuffed mini peppers

Calories: 115

Protein: 4 g

Carbohydrates: 25 g

Sugar: 13 g

Fat: 1 g

Calories from fat: 5%

Fiber: 5 g

Sodium: 429 mg

Ingredients

- 4 mini paprika's
- 1 to 2 spring onions
- Fresh peppers (chili)
- Garlic (fresh or dried)
- 4 anchovy fillets (cut into fine pieces)
- 1 tomato
- Olives
- Parsley

- Capers or caper apple
- Chapelure, breadcrumbs or panko
- 100 gr goat cheese or feta

Preparation

1. Traeger setting: maximum heat
2. Prepare the filling in advance: finely chop everything, mix together to a grainy filling.
3. Cut the vegetables in half lengthwise, remove the seeds. Spread the edges with a little oil and place it on the concave side on the hot spot in the traeger. (usually at the back of the grill)
4. Lightly color the edges of the vegetables. Then take it back from the traeger and fill it with the filling.
5. Place the stuffed peppers back on the grill and cook for about 5-10 minutes. (does not have to be well done)

Baked tomato with herb butter

Calories: 115

Protein: 4 g

Carbohydrates: 25 g

Sugar: 13 g

Fat: 1 g

Fiber: 5 g

Sodium: 429 mg

Ingredients

- 1 tomato per person (not too big)
- Pepper and salt
- Herb butter
- Breadcrumbs or panko (chinese breadcrumbs / fine bread flakes)
- Sprinkle cheese
- Aluminum shell

Preparation

1. Remove the crown and halve the tomatoes.
2. Season with salt and pepper.
3. Place a slice of herb butter both each half tomato.
4. Finish with breadcrumbs.
5. Place in an aluminum bowl.

6. Set your traeger to 176 ° c and place the aluminum tray on the grill.
7. Bake for 8 to 12 minutes (according to the size of the tomatoes and the number of tomatoes in the aluminum dish)

Tips

When the peel of the tomatoes bursts, they are just a little overcooked. This is avoided by using the aluminum shell: because only the seasoned side is exposed to the direct heat, the peel layer will therefore be less likely to crack.

Tasty!

Grilled asparagus

Calories: 111

Protein: 5 g

Carbohydrates: 26 g

Fat: 2 g

Fiber: 5 g

Sodium: 429 mg

Ingredients

- Water - 1 glass
- Fresh asparagus - 450 g
- Bbq sauce - 1/4 cup

Preparation

1. In a big skillet, bring 1 cup water to a boil. Put the asparagus in boiling water, cover the pan with a lid and blanch the asparagus for about 4-6 minutes, until completely soft. Remove the asparagus from the water and transfer to a paper towel, blot well to remove all liquid.
2. Soak wooden skewers into cold water for 5 minutes so that they do not burn during frying. Turn on the grill to preheat to medium heat.

3. String the cooled asparagus on wooden skewers (as shown in the photo).
4. Place the asparagus on the grill rack and cook, uncovered, for about 1 minute on each side. Then brush the asparagus with barbecue sauce and cook for about 2 minutes more, turn over, grease the other side with the sauce and cook for about 1 minute.
5. Serve the asparagus immediately.

Grilled stuffed bell pepper

Ingredients

- Olive oil - 1/2 cup + 2 tsp.
- Parmesan cheese (shredded on a greater) - 3/4 cup
- Fresh basil leaves - 2 cups
- Sunflower seeds (kernels) or walnuts (kernels) - 2 tbsp.
- Garlic - 4 cloves
- Bulgarian pepper (seeded and finely chopped) - 1/2 cup
- Corn grains (canned) - 4 cups
- Medium sized bulgarian pepper - 4 pcs.
- Parmesan cheese (grated) (for serving) - 1/4 cup

Preparation

1. Switch on the grill to preheat to medium temperature.
2. Prepare the pesto sauce. Pour 1/2 cup olive oil inside the bowl of a food processor or blender, add 3/4 cup cheese, basil, seeds (or nuts) and garlic, pulsate until smooth.
3. In a large skillet, then heat the remaining olive oil; add the chopped bell pepper and fry, stirring occasionally, until soft. Add corn and pesto to the pan and stir well.
4. Cut a whole bell pepper into halves, remove seeds and stalks. Place the halves on a preheated grill, slices down. Place your lid on the grill and cook the

peppers for about 8 minutes. Then stuff the pepper halves with the corn mixture and grill for another 4-6 minutes, until the pepper is soft.
5. Serve the finished dish sprinkled with parmesan.

Zucchini cutlets

Calories: 115

Protein: 4 g

Carbohydrates: 25 g

Sugar: 13 g

Fat: 1 g

Fiber: 5 g

Sodium: 429 mg

Ingredients

- Zucchini - 750 g
- Salt and black pepper
- Egg (slightly beaten) - 1 pc.
- Coarse flour - 2/3 cup (60 g)
- Chopped nutmeg - 1/4 tsp.

For the sauce:

- Lemon zest - 1 tsp
- Lemon juice - 1 tbsp.
- Mint (chopped) - 3-4 tbsp.
- Fat-free yogurt (natural) - 150 g

Preparation

1. Grind the zucchini with a blender or on a fine grater, season with salt, leave for 30 minutes at room temperature. Then rinse inside a colander under running cold water. Squeeze well with your hands and put on a paper towel, blot.
2. Transfer the chopped zucchini to a bowl and add the egg, flour, nutmeg and pepper. Mix everything well and let it brew at room temperature for 20 minutes.
3. Prepare the sauce. In a separate bowl, combine lemon, zest, mint and yogurt. Cover and refrigerate.
4. Heat a skillet or skillet over medium heat. Spoon the zucchini mixture (1 tablespoon each) into the pan and gently form the patties. Fry for 3-4 minutes on each side. Serve with yoghurt sauce.

Fried eggplant with tomato sauce

Ingredients

- Eggplant - 2 pcs.
- Olive oil - 4 tbsp.
- Garlic - 2 cloves
- Paprika - ½ tsp.
- Sea salt
- Black pepper, freshly ground
- Tomatoes (canned, cut into pieces) - 400 g

Preparation

1. Preheat a barbecue or cast iron grill pan with ribbed bottom. Cut the eggplants into 1 cm circles and place in a colander. Sprinkle with salt, press down with a plate and let sit for 15 minutes. Rinse and then pat dry using a paper towel.
2. Preheat 1 tbsp. L. Butter in a skillet over low heat. Add the sliced garlic and paprika. Cook it for a few seconds, salt and pepper. Stir in the tomato pulp, bring to a boil over high heat, reduce heat and simmer for 15 minutes.
3. Brush the eggplant using the remaining oil and grill on a barbecue or skillet for 3 minutes on each side, until golden brown. Pour over cooked tomato sauce and serve.
4. Enjoy your meal!

Grilled vegetables with herbs

Ingredients

- Young zucchini - 2 pcs, young eggplants - 2 pcs, bulb onions - 2 pcs.
- Bulgarian pepper - 3 pcs, tomatoes - 4 pcs, chili peppers - 4 pcs.

For the marinade:

- Olive oil - 3-4 tbsp. Spoons, hops-suneli - 2 tsp
- Dried thyme - 2 tsp, freshly ground black pepper - to taste
- Salt to taste

Preparation

1. Cut the eggplants into circles. I prefer to cut them thicker - about one and a half to two centimeters. Cut the zucchini in the same way.
2. Peel the onions. And cut into circles. With him, too, "small" is not necessary. Put onions on skewers so that the rings do not fall apart when grilling.
3. So that the skewers are not too long and do not interfere with cooking, I cut them with a pruner.
4. Remove the core out from the bell pepper, and then cut it into 4 pieces.
5. Tomatoes don't need any special preparation; they just need to be washed. Do the same with red chili peppers.

6. Let's move on to preparing a mixture for pickling vegetables. In a deep bowl, mix the suneli hops, thyme, salt and freshly ground pepper. Pour the spices with olive oil. Mix the contents of the bowl.
7. Transfer vegetables to a deep bowl. Fill them with a mixture of oil and aromatic herbs. Distribute the mixture over the whole surface of the vegetables (except for tomatoes and chili peppers - we will not marinate them, because we did not cut the skin in any way, and the marinade simply will not penetrate inside). Leave the vegetables to marinate for 15 minutes.
8. Grilling coals. While preparing the grill, another 10-15 minutes passed, which means that the vegetables were completely marinated. Not immediately, already in a slight heat, without fear that they will burn, spread the vegetables on the grill. After about 4-5 minutes, turn the vegetables over and grill for the same amount of time.

Grilled potatoes and tomatoes

Calories: 125

Protein: 12 g

Carbohydrates: 25 g

Sugar: 13 g

Calories from fat: 5%

Fiber: 5 g

Ingredients

- Young potatoes - 900 g
- White wine vinegar - 1 tsp
- Olive oil - 7 tbsp.
- Chives inflorescences (chopped) - 45 g (3 tbsp. L.)
- Cream tomatoes, yellow - 4-5 pcs.
- Salt and black pepper to taste

Preparation

1. Switch on the grill to preheat to medium temperature. Boil the potatoes in lightly salted water until soft, for about 10 minutes.
2. Meanwhile, prepare the tomato and potato dressing. In a small bowl, combine chives, wine vinegar and

5 tablespoons of olive oil. Throw boiled potatoes in a colander, let the water drain, and then cut each tuber lengthwise, in half. Add salt and pepper to taste.
3. When the grill is hot, take the potatoes one half at a time, dip the slices in the remaining oil and place them on the wire shelf, cut side down. Fry for about 5 minutes.
4. Turn potato halves over and fry for about 3 minutes. Place the fried potatoes in a large bowl, drizzle with the dressing and stir.
5. Place the tomato halves on the wire rack and fry for 3 minutes.
6. Serve potatoes with tomatoes.

Sweet potato salad

Ingredients

For the salad:

- Small sweet potato - 1 kg
- Pea leaves mung bean - 140 g
- Soft cheese (crumbled) - 1 glass
- Dried caramelized cranberries - 1/2 cup
- Vegetable oil
- Chili pepper (seeded and finely chopped) - 1 pc.
- Pumpkin seeds (roasted, peeled) - 1/2 cup

For refueling:

- Red wine vinegar - 1/4 cup
- Fresh cilantro (chopped) - 2 tbsp.
- Salad onion (chopped) - 2 tbsp.
- Fresh ginger (chopped on a grater) - 1 tbsp.
- Liquid honey - 2 tbsp.
- Orange peel - 2 tsp
- Dijon mustard - 2 tsp
- Salt - 1/2 tsp.
- Vegetable oil - 1/2 cup

Preparation

1. Prepare the dressing. In a small bowl combine vinegar, cilantro, onion, ginger, honey, orange zest, mustard and salt, mix well, then add oil and mix well again. Set aside.
2. Prepare salad. Grease the grill grate with vegetable oil, and turn on the grill for preheating to medium-high temperature (180-200 degrees).
3. Peel off sweet potato and cut into slices about 1.2 centimeters thick. Boil sweet potatoes in water until soft and cartilage, for about 5-6 minutes. Dry and brush with vegetable oil.
4. Place the sweet potatoes on the grill, cover the grill and fry the sweet potatoes on both sides (only 8-10 minutes) until tender. Toss the fried sweet potatoes in a large bowl with the chili and the dressing.
5. Put green mung bean leaves on a serving dish, sprinkle with cheese and cranberries. Put potatoes on mung bean and sprinkle pumpkin seeds on the sweet potato salad.
6. Serve the sweet potato salad immediately.

Grilled green peas and champignons

Ingredients

- Green peas - 450 g
- Fresh champignon mushrooms (sliced) - 1/2 cup
- Green onions (chopped) - 2 tbsp.
- Fresh dill (finely chopped) - 1 tbsp.
- Butter - 2 tbsp.
- Salt and black pepper to taste

Preparation

1. Switch on the grill to preheat to medium temperature. Put the peas and mushrooms in a heat-resistant mold (or a homemade foil mold). Sprinkle mushrooms and peas with dill and onions, top with butter, cut into small pieces. Cover the form with a lid or wrap in foil.
2. Place the dish with vegetables on the grill rack, cover the grill with the lid and cook the dish for about 5-8 minutes, then stir the vegetables and cook for about 5 more minutes, until mushrooms and peas are soft. Season the dish with few salt and pepper to taste before serving.

Grilled vegetables and mushrooms

Ingredients

- Olive oil - 1/2 cup
- Red wine vinegar - 1/4 cup
- Fresh oregano (finely chopped) 1 tbsp.
- Dijon mustard - 1 tbsp
- Garlic (peeled and minced) - 2 cloves
- Salt - 1/2 tsp.
- Ground black pepper - 1/4 tsp.
- Medium green zucchini (cut into thick circles) - 4 pcs.
- Medium yellow zucchini (cut into thick circles) - 4 pcs.
- Medium-sized red onions (peeled off and cut into quarters) - 2 pcs.
- Red bulgarian pepper (peeled from seeds and cut into pieces) - 1 pc.
- Bulgarian yellow pepper (peeled from seeds and cut into pieces) - 1 pc.
- Fresh champignons - 12-16 pcs.
- Cherry tomatoes - 12 pcs.

Preparation

1. In a small bowl, add vinegar, oil, oregano, mustard, garlic, salt and black pepper, beat with a whisk or fork (you can do this in a special shaker).
2. Put all the prepared vegetables into a deep bowl, pour the marinade, mix well, leave to marinate at room temperature for 15 minutes.
3. Switch on the grill to preheat to medium temperature. Remove the vegetables from the marinade and place on the oiled grill rack. Place the lid on the grill and then cook for about 10-12 minutes, until the vegetables are soft.

Grilled cabbage rolls

Ingredients

- Chinese cabbage - 1 large head of cabbage
- Rice (dry) - 3/4 cup
- Canned corn - 1 can
- Peeled peanuts - 0.5 cups
- Dill greens - 2 tbsp. Spoons
- Vegetable oil - 1 tbsp. The spoon
- Salt
- Ketchup

Preparation

1. Disassemble the cabbage into leaves and put it in hot water for 1 minute. Remove, cool and cut off the thickenings, placing the knife almost horizontally. Cook crumbly porridge from rice. Rinse the rice. Fry the peanuts.
2. For the filling, combine rice, strained corn, chopped dill and peanuts. It may be better to chop the peanuts. Salt everything to taste.
3. Place a full tablespoon of filling on the prepared peking cabbage leaves and wrap.
4. Fry cabbage rolls on both sides on a greased grill. If you fry them well, then the cabbage rolls will be ready. If there is no grill, you can fry the cabbage rolls in an ordinary pan.
5. But if you don't want to fry too much. Put the cabbage rolls in a baking sheet, pour them with

ketchup and put the lean cabbage rolls in the oven for 15 minutes at 170 degrees.

Grilled ajapsandal (ajapsandali)

Ingredients

- Eggplant - 2 pcs.
- Tomatoes - 4 pcs.
- Bulgarian pepper - 2 pcs.
- Bulb onions - 1 pc.
- Garlic - 4 cloves
- Fresh basil - 1 bunch
- Fresh parsley - 1 bunch
- Salt to taste

Preparation

1. We send two eggplants and an onion to the grill. Close with a lid and then leave for 5 minutes. After 5 minutes, turn the vegetables over and again leave them to fry for another 5 minutes. Do not be afraid that the vegetables will burn. There is nothing wrong with that, because we will cleanse them of burnt skin.
2. Spread bell peppers and tomatoes on the grill. Let them cook for 5 minutes on each side, then remove the vegetables from the grill.

3. All baked vegetables are peeled and cut into arbitrary, not very large pieces.
4. Finely chop the garlic cloves. Finely chop the basil and parsley greens.
5. Place all vegetables and herbs in a salad bowl and mix the ajapsandali properly. Don't forget to add salt.
6. Enjoy your meal!

Zucchini ragout with carrots and onions on the grill

Ingredients

- Zucchini - 1.3 kg
- Carrots - 200 g
- Onions - 100 g
- Tomato paste - 3 tbsps. Spoons
- Salt to taste
- Ground black pepper - to taste

Preparation

1. Peel off the onion and cut into medium cubes.
2. Peel the carrots and cut into medium cubes.
3. Peel the zucchini and cut into medium cubes.
4. We send chopped zucchini, onions, and carrots to a bowl. Add tomato paste. Salt and pepper to taste.
5. Mix everything thoroughly. We prepare a foil about 70x70 cm in size (we overlap three sheets with a length of 70 cm). Stepping back 5-10 cm from the edge spread the mixture of vegetables on the foil.
6. We wrap the vegetables in foil and send them to the wire rack.
7. Pour coal on the grill and light the fire. When the coals are burned out, pour water over the flame so that there is no open fire.

8. Put the grill with vegetables in foil on the grill. Cooking zucchini with carrots and onions on the grill for 1.5 hours, turning every 20 minutes.
9. Serve the vegetable stew in foil to preserve the vegetable juice.

Grilled zucchini

Ingredients

- Zucchini - 2 pcs. (500 g)
- Lemon juice - 2 tbsp. Spoons
- Sweet mustard - 1 tsp
- Garlic - 3 cloves
- Olive oil - 2-3 tbsp. Spoons
- Sugar - 0.5 tsp
- Dried greens - 2 pinches
- Salt to taste
- Ground black pepper - to taste

Preparation

1. Cut the courgettes at an angle into equal sized slices.
2. Prepare the marinade. To do this, put mustard in a bowl and add lemon juice.
3. Finely chop those garlic with a knife and add to the marinade.

4. Pour in dried herbs and sugar. Add salt and black pepper.
5. Pour in olive oil and whisk the marinade well until it thickens and turns slightly white. Put the zucchini in a bag, preferably in a bag with a fastener.
6. Pour the marinade into the bag to the zucchini. Close the package.
7. Mix the zucchini well with the marinade and leave to marinate for 2 hours. Then fry the zucchini in a grill pan for 3-5 minutes on one side.
8. Turn the zucchini over and fry for the same amount of time on the other side.
9. Grilled courgettes are ready. Such zucchini will be an excellent side dish for meat or fish, but they are also good as an independent dish.
10. Enjoy your meal!

Grilled vegetables

Calories: 115

Protein: 4 g

Carbohydrates: 25 g

Sugar: 13 g

Fat: 1 g

Sodium: 429 mg

Ingredients

- Zucchini - 1 pc.
- Eggplant - 1-2 pcs.
- Tomato - 1-2 pcs.
- Corn (boiled) - 1-2 pcs.
- Bulgarian pepper - 1 pc.
- Bulb onions – optional
- Vegetable oil - 2 tbsp. Spoons
- Salt to taste

Preparation

1. Prepare the required ingredients for your grilled vegetables. Rinse vegetables in water. Boil corn cobs in boiling salted water for about 10 minutes.
2. How to grill vegetables: cut the tails of zucchini and eggplants; cut them into plates no more than 0.5 cm thick. Peel the bell pepper from seeds, cut into ribbons.
3. Preheat an electric grill and brush it with vegetable oil, or heat a charcoal grill. If you cook on charcoal, then salt the vegetables in advance and brush with vegetable oil.
4. Place zucchini and eggplant slices and pepper strips on the grill. If you have a double-pan technique, then close the grill and fry the vegetables for 2-3 minutes. If not, flip them over to the other side after 1-2 minutes.
5. Once the previous slices are cooked through, place them on a plate and place the boiled corn and sliced tomato on the grill.
6. Fry the same amount of time until the characteristic stripes.
7. Place the baked tomatoes and corn with the rest of the grilled vegetables on a plate. Serve colorful chunks of grilled vegetables with any sauce of your choice: mayonnaise, tartar, thick yogurt, sour cream, aioli, etc.

Grilled vegetables with butter sauce

Ingredients

- 2 onions
- 4 mini eggplants
- 4 mini pumpkins
- 2 corns, 2 tomatoes
- 200 g mushrooms
- 8 asparagus
- 1 head of garlic

For sauce:

- 100 gr butter, 25 g stuffed peanuts
- 2 tablespoons lemon juice
- 2 cloves of crushed garlic
- 2 sprigs of fresh thyme
- 2 sprigs of fresh basil
- 1 teaspoon of red paprika
- 1 teaspoon black pepper
- Salt

Preparation

1. For the sauce, soften the butter at room temperature, lean fried peanuts, lemon juice, garlic, spices and salt in a lean pan and take it to the blender until smooth.
2. Cut the vegetables to a desired size and put them on the heated grill. Apply the sauce prepared with a

brush. Cook until golden brown and put on a serving plate. Serve hot.

Eggplant salad with spinach grill

Ingredients

- 1 piece of eggplant sliced and sliced
- 1/8 cup of mint leaves only
- 1/2 bunch of parsley leaves only
- 1 tablespoon of oregano
- 1/4 cup of dehydrated tomato cut in thirds
- 4 cups fresh baby spinach
- 2 cloves garlic, finely chopped, for dressing
- 1 tablespoon of tahini for dressing
- 1/2 tablespoon paprika for dressing
- 1 piece of lemon juice, for dressing
- 1 tablespoon olive oil for dressing
- 1 pinch of salt for dressing
- 1/4 cup of crumbled feta cheese

Preparation

1. Heat a grill above high heat; grill the aubergines until the classic grill marks are formed. Withdraw and reserve
2. In a bowl mix the aubergines with the mint leaves, the parsley, the oregano, the dehydrated tomatoes, and the spinach. Reservation.
3. In a bowl, mix the garlic, tahini, paprika, lemon and olive oil with the balloon whisk and season to your liking.
4. Mix the salad with the dressing and sprinkle to your liking with the feta cheese.

Vegan vegetable kebabs with herbs

Vegan vegetable skewers with herbs are the perfect alternative for those who want to barbecue meatless or even look for a delicious vegetable garnish.

Ingredients

- 200 g cherry tomatoes
- 100 g of zucchini
- 100 g of radish
- 100 g paprika
- 100 g mushrooms
- 1 onion
- 1 sprig of rosemary
- 2 sprigs of thyme
- 3 tbsp. Olive oil
- Colorful pepper
- Sea-salt

Preparation

1. Wash the tomatoes and radishes and drain
2. Cut the zucchini into thick slices and divide into 4 pieces
3. Free the radish from the green and cut in half
4. For peppers, remove the cores and partitions, rinse and cut into pieces.
5. Peel the onion and cut into pieces

6. Wash the herbs and shake them dry, then pluck the leaves from the stalk and chop
7. Clean the mushrooms and cut off the dry stem end
8. Then cut the mushrooms in half.

Mediterranean grilled vegetables with lemon yoghurt dressing and potatoes

Ingredients

- Garlic
- Tomatoes
- Onion
- Vegetables
- Potatoes
- Yoghurt
- Water
- Lemon juice
- Salt and pepper
- Rosemary sprigs

Preparation

1. Wash the small potatoes and then pre-cook in boiling salted water for 8 minutes. Drain the potatoes and cut in half. Clean the vegetables and cut into pieces. Remove the onion and diced. Peel

off the garlic clove and chop finely. Wash the date tomatoes, but leave them alone.
2. Now put the potatoes, the chopped vegetables, tomatoes, onions and garlic in a baking dish. Season with salt and add pepper, add the rosemary sprigs and mix again. Give olive oil over it.
3. Heat the air fryer to 260 ° c grill function, insert the casserole dish and grill the vegetables for about 15 minutes.
4. Meanwhile mix together the yoghurt, the light mayonnaise and the lemon juice and season with salt and pepper.
5. The yoghurt dressing for mediterranean grilled vegetables is enough. The grilled vegetables with the potatoes taste both warm and cold. Therefore, it is also ideal for party buffets or takeaway!

Grilled fruits with caramel sauce

Calories: 115

Protein: 4 g

Carbohydrates: 25 g

Ingredients

For the fruit kebabs:

- 2 apples, 1 mango
- 1/2 pineapple
- 8 strawberries
- 1/2 lemon

1 tbsp. Sugar for the caramel sauce:

- 150 g butter
- 70 g of sugar
- 100 ml whipped cream

Preparation

1. Peel the apples for the grilled fruit, cut into slices, removing the core casing. Peel the mango, remove the core and cut into slices or cubes. Peel the pineapple, remove the woody interior and cut into cubes. Wash the strawberries, remove leaf green.

2. Squeeze out the lemon. Sprinkle the fruit with lemon juice and sprinkle with sugar. Alternately place the pieces of fruit on wooden skewers and grill on the hot grill for approx. 6 minutes, turning frequently. Melt the butter and brush the fruit skewers with the melted butter over and over while grilling. Do not leave the skewers on your grill too long so that the fruit pieces do not get muddy.
3. For the caramel sauce, put butter and sugar in a saucepan and melt. Stir till the sugar become dissolved and it turned brown. Heat whipped cream in air fryer and stir in the caramel.
4. The grilled fruits serve with caramel sauce.

Tips

the recipe for the grilled fruit can make you a little more substantial by brushing the fruits while grilling with white wine or sherry.

Grilled zucchini salad

Ingredient

- 2 zucchini
- 3 tablespoons mild olive oil
- 1 tbsp balsamic vinegar
- 50 g of hazelnuts
- 15 g fresh basil
- 10 g of fresh mint
- 150 g burrata

Preparation

1. Cut the zucchini into 1 cm long slices. Season with salt and pepper and sprinkle with olive oil, heat the grill pan and grill the zucchini slices in 4 minutes. Turn halfway. Put the zucchini slices in a bowl, mix with the balsamic vinegar and let stand until use.
2. Heat up a pan without oil or butter and roast the hazelnuts until golden brown for 3 minutes over medium heat. Cool on a plate and chop roughly.
3. Cut basil leaves and mint roughly. The stems of basil finely chop, they have a lot of taste. Mix the zucchini with the herbs and the rest of the oil. Tear the burrata to pieces.
4. Divide first the zucchini and then the burrata over the plates. Sprinkle with the roasted hazelnuts and herbs - season with (freshly ground) pepper and possibly salt.

Avocado wrapped in bacon

Ingredients

- 2 avocados (ripe)
- 15-20 strips of bacon

Preparation

1. For the avocado wrapped in bacon wrapped in bacon, first, preheat the oven to 180 ° c. Cover a baking tray with baking paper.
2. Halve the avocado and remove the kernel. Carefully remove the pulp (preferably with a tablespoon). Then cut lengthwise into approximately 1 cm thick slits.
3. Wrap each column with a strip of bacon and place on the baking sheet. Put the avocado wrapped in bacon in the oven for about 15 minutes until the bacon is crispy. Best observe because every oven is a little different.

Tips

the bacon-wrapped avocado is ideal as a starter, snack, or side dish. It can also be prepared as a grill on the grill.

SOME INFORMATION

Instructions

Please read the manual. Follow all security restrictions on the letter. If you have a fever and you didn't follow the instructions, whatever happens, that's your fault. You must know these before enlightenment. Don't assume your new grid works like the last and the same rules apply. One tip: you can find guides to most grills and smokers on the manufacturer's website.

Coal safety

Charcoal grills are the cause of much more fire than gas grills. The number one problem with the charcoal grill is lighting the charcoal. Lighter liquid causes all sorts of problems and you should find a better way to light your coals. What really burns your facial hair is adding lighter fluid to the hot coals. The lighter liquid becomes a heavy gas at a relatively low temperature. Vaporized (gaseous) lighter fluid explodes while liquid lighter fluid is burning. Flow the instructions exactly and don't let the lighting charcoal be a game.

Duman

Smoke gets on your hair, clothes, eyes and lungs. While a large part of the cooking experience is smoke, you should be mindful of this. Your grill or smoker smoke contains carbon monoxide, polycyclic aromatic hydrocarbons (pah) and other hazardous substances.

Gas safety

The main cause of gas grill fires is a blockage in the fuel path. This largely happens under, behind, under or inside the grill that you are not looking at. This means you should check your gas grills regularly. Bugs and other critics can climb into small places causing the gas to not flow. Turn off your check readings at the first sign of problems, close the fuel tank and disconnect everything. Gas grills generate large amounts of heat that can melt between hoses, buttons and other parts. Suppose everything is third degree hot burn.

Gres

It's not bad enough that you are using flammable ingredients for cooking, but food creates more. Flares are more than a nuisance, they are potentially deadly. Fats accumulated in the grill form over time. It's easy to grab a few pounds of grease on the bottom of your grill after just a few cooks. That's why you need to keep your grill clean.

Place

Location is everything when it comes to grill or smoker placement. Hundreds of people fire on their homes, garages and courtyards every year because they didn't put their grills or smokers in the right place. Take care of your equipment and imagine the worst fire you could ever do. Make sure there is nothing (building, tree, etc.) In that area. Also, make sure that your grills do not want people to get too close to hot surfaces and children to play nearby.

Cancer

Cooking (by any method) meats (especially red meat and chicken) can produce cancer-causing substances (heterocyclic amines (hca)) at very high temperatures until surface tingling occurs. To minimize the risk you should do:

- use marinades (can reduce risk by up to 98%)

- excessive foods

- keep grill temperatures relatively low (cooking temperature below 600 degrees)

- use thinner or less meat cutting (kebabs are great)

Alcohol

Grilling and smoking need clear thought, especially when it's time to put it all together. Please keep a clean head and store it after setting that drink on fire and after someone else washes the dishes.

Grill

The grill is the cooking system in which the food rests on bars, of different shapes and sizes and, under these, the fuel in the form of firewood or coal heats at the same time the iron and the food that, little by little, is cooking.

A very important aspect to consider when choosing a grill is the type of bar that can be round, in v or square.

The round bar is the most generous with the product, since when falling on the embers the fat of the product that we are cooking generates a smoke that aromatizes it. It is true that this can raise flame, but if we know how to handle it, the result is superior from the gastronomic point of view.

The v-bar, on the other hand, is easier to handle, since it picks up the fat that releases the food to a grease trap and it is more difficult for flames to be generated, but instead we lose in aromas. It is a system that is widely used in hospitality, since it allows cooking more quickly and without problems, but does not make much sense for a domestic grill.

Also, the square bar is similar from the gastronomic point of view to the round. It is very popular in the united states, but in Europe it is difficult to find it.

Apart from the type of bar, which can be chosen in most models, there are fixed, semi-fixed and portable grills.

If we have a large garden we may be interested in installing a work grill , which can be found in different sizes from 100 euros (although a good one, for 5 or 6 people, does not fall below 300). These are models whose installation is more complex, but they are a good option in country houses where there is adequate space to install it. However, these are less versatile instruments and whose purchase is made almost as a function of the available space.

The semi - fixed grills are prefabricated structures designed to cram in a reserved space for these. They usually also have a drawer to collect the ashes. It is a good option if there is adequate space to install it and we do not want to get involved with a grille, much more expensive.

THE BARBECUE

The barbecue season begins and, with it, the doubts about where to do these. As is currently the case with most of the utensils, the price range goes from practically zero to thousands of dollars/euros, but there are several intermediate options, relatively affordable, that are worth considering for our home. Investing in a good barbecue allows us to enjoy grilled cuisine in more circumstances than we think and in a much more comfortable way, but to choose the model that best suits our needs we must first learn to distinguish the different types that exist well, in fact, not even barbecue and grill are synonymous in this the world of embers.

The barbecue is simply a grill with a lid, an additive that at first glance may not be decisive but that makes the invention a much more complex kitchen system, because, if it is lowered, it transforms it into an oven that cooks food from controlled form. Also, thanks to the lid, the barbecue serves to smoke food, both cold and hot, and makes the instrument much safer, because if you have to leave the fire for any reason just lower this and close the shot to stay calm.

The barbecue is, in fact, a relatively recent invention. In 1950, George Stephen, known as the Newton of the barbecues, made a party to inaugurate his new house, he did not know how to control the fire of his work grill and the food was scorched. That was when he thought about creating an improved grill.

There is nothing like cooking open flame food. The techniques are simple, cleaning is easy and grilled food tastes amazing.

Turn on the barbecue, choose the recipe you like best and use this guide as a manual to get started.

1. Choose a grill

Grill purists agree that charcoal gives food flavor, but the comfort and speed of gas grills has made them the most popular option for homemade barbecues.

Charcoal grills are ideal for tighter budgets and when you have time to wait for it to turn on, but you have to clean more and get dirtier. Propane gas grills require a 75-liter tank of propane and ignite at the touch of a button. Some gas grills can also be installed in such a way that they work with household gas, so the tank is no longer needed. You can give more flavor to the food if you place a piece of mesquite or cherry wood on the barbecue while everything is cooking, which will enhance that flavor.

2. Prepare the space

It is convenient to have a side table to prepare the food while you place it on the grill. Many barbecues carry a small side table and possibly a kind of additional stove to cook food in a pan or pot, as well as food that you make on the grill. Try to have a clear area to leave the food tray and leave any accessories you need such as the brush, tweezers and thermometer. A light is also useful when cooking at night.

3. Select a meal

Three things must be taken into account when grilling food. The first is if you are going to use direct or indirect heat, the second is how hot the grill should be and the third is how long you should cook the food. You can also choose to grill with or without a lid, which regulates the temperature.

Just as you preheat the oven, you have to preheat the grill before cooking. Regardless of the temperature at which you cook, it is best to preheat the barbecue at high temperature and then lower it to the configuration you need.

Pour a thin layer of grilled cooking oil while it warms to prevent food from sticking.

Cow meat

Steaks, hamburgers and hot dogs are common grilled foods, and all beef products should usually be cooked over direct heat with the grill at their height. In hot dogs and thin fillets, the heat can be reduced slightly.

In less than 10 minutes, steaks and burgers are ready so that they do not get confused or harder than a sole shoe. After removing the steak from the grill, the steak needs time to "rest" so let it sit down with foil for approximately five minutes.

Professional advice: try to mark the meat to get steaks cooked uniformly, tenderly and deliciously. Make shallow cuts (about 4 cm) on one side and then on the other side with a sharp knife tip (perpendicular to the first cuts). On the other hand, repeat. Savor the steak and roast for 1 or 2 minutes less on each side over medium-high heat.

Chicken

Roasting chicken takes a little longer and should be done at medium temperature. It is easy for the chicken to dry out on the grill, so it is better to cook it slowly and leave it in brine overnight or apply a marinade or sauce to keep it moist. Indirect heat is best for boneless chicken; give it at least 30-40 minutes to cook. Always use the meat thermometer to know when it's ready.

Pork

Roasting pork is similar to beef, uses direct heat, but lowers the heat over medium heat. Pork chops can be cooked quickly and, depending on the thickness, it only takes 2-4 minutes on each side.

Professional advice: use a meat thermometer! Cutting the meat to make sure it is made, makes all the juice come out and dismount. And, more importantly, it is not as accurate a method as using a thermometer. When the meat is ready to be removed from the grill, it is not yet ready to be consumed. Letting it rest for certain minutes helps seal those juices.

Seafood

The fish cook very well on the grill and do not leave the kitchen with a strange smell. Use medium to medium-high direct heat and plenty of oil to prevent fish from sticking. Fish and shellfish are also cooked well wrapped in foil with butter and seasonings, which prevents the fish from sticking to the grill.

Seafood is grilled in less than 8 minutes, and prawns are a quick and tasty meal whatever the size of the grill.

Vegetables

With a gas barbecue you can grill asparagus, eggplant and zucchini, next to the steak or chicken, just try to make the fire medium and be careful to quickly remove the vegetables, since it is very easy to burn. Olive oil, salt and pepper, you don't need any more condiments to prepare your vegetables.

4. Cleaning

Proper cleaning is key to making your next barbecue a success. Use a metal brush immediately after cooking to remove excess oil and bits of food. Keeping the grill racks clean prevents the accumulation of bacteria, deters insects and pests and also prevents the accumulation of coal that could eventually alter the operation of the barbecue.

Cover the grill when you do not use it, so you will protect it from the elements and prolong its life.

SUMMARY AND CONCLUSION

Beyond the choice of meat, there are some factors that must be taken into account when preparing the barbecue. When roasting the food directly on the flames or embers, it is common to form a roasted surface layer that can be harmful to health. They are called "heterocyclic amines", carcinogenic components that appear when a food is exposed to high temperatures. In case of cooking wide-cut meats and to prevent that blackish crust from forming, it is recommended to pre-cook it for a few minutes in the oven or less than 60 seconds in the microwave before you take it to the grill. With this, it is achieved that the exposure of the food to the heat of the embers is less, according to the graduate in nutrition and member of the association of dietitians-nutritionists of Madridluján Soler Santoro. "if the food gets too hot, it could also lose its nutritional and organoleptic properties (taste, smell, texture, color).

In addition to meat or fish, this nutritionist advises adding vegetables and fruits to follow the recommendation of the world health organization to consume a minimum of 5 pieces per day (about 400 grams). "tomatoes, asparagus, peppers, eggplants, zucchini or onions are some of the vegetables that will provide a good dose of minerals," he says.

As for the dressing, the healthiest is a mixture of oil, garlic and raw spices, which will accompany the meat or fish once roasted.

If you have already decided on a healthy barbecue, it is important that you write down these recommendations of the consumers and users organization :

Hygiene guarantees

1. Try that the meat has spent as much time as possible in the fridge, especially if you bought it on a day with high temperatures. If you have to move, a good option is isothermal bags and portable refrigerators.

2. Don't forget to wash hands well before handling food.

3. Avoid cross contamination by using different cutlery for raw and cooked meat.

4. Has something left over? Put it into your fridge as soon as possible.

5. If you think that the barbecue has not cooked enough meat, do not hesitate to give it one more pass through the pan or oven.

Security guarantees

1. Stay away from anything that can burn.

2. Always carry out the outdoor barbecue.

3. Watch it permanently. Do not let children get close.

4. Mount it on a flat surface.

5. Be careful to get too close. In coal barbecues the contact temperature can reach 100 degrees.

6. Never use alcohol or gasoline to light it. Always specific pills or gels.

7. Wait until the flames have disappeared to place the food. On the coals there should be a layer of white ash.

8. If using a charcoal barbecue, place the grill at least 10 centimeters above the coals.

9. Turn off heat as soon as you finish eating.

10. Always have a bucket of water nearby. It will help you in case of an accident.